ACTA UNIVERSITATIS UPSALIENSIS
Studia Iuridica Upsaliensia
7

QMC

a 30

D0543957

WITHDRAWN
FROM STOCK
QMUL LIBRARY

The Non-Contractual and Contractual Liability of the European Communities

Göran Lysén

UPPSALA 1976

Distributor:
Almqvist & Wiksell International
Stockholm

Doctoral thesis at Uppsala University 1976

176930
KM 19

ISBN 91—554—0406—5
ISSN 0562—2832

QUEEN MARY COLLEGE
LIBRARY
MILE END ROAD,
LONDON, E.1.

©Göran Lysén 1976

Printed in Sweden 1976
TEXTgruppen i uppsala ab

To
Christina and Hans Fredrik

Table of Contents

Part one
Notes on the Legal Framework of the European Communities

Chapter one
The institutions and some community organs

Chapter two
The Court of Justice

Chapter three
The Sources of community law

Part two
The Non-Contractual Liability of the Communities

Chapter four
General points concerning community liability

Part three

The Contractual Liability of the Communities

Acknowledgements

The idea of making a profound study into a community topic arose in my mind after attending a course in 1972 concerning the European Common Market at the University of Stockholm held by Professor G O Zacharias Sundström with whom I later had the pleasure of working for more than one year in his law offices as an associated lawyer. In deciding on the topic the problem was not in finding anything interesting concerning the Communities but in choosing the subject. I made up my mind in the beginning of 1973 and then proceeded to work.

In this context I would like to thank my family for always being encouraging and in particular my wife who also assisted me in prepairing the book lists, abbreviations and case-law not to mention the extensive typing she has helped me with. I would also like to give my thanks to the European Commission which granted me a trainee period of six months in 1973—1974 in its Directorate-General for the Internal Market where I actively participated in the work of European Integration and studied it on the spot. Here I wish to give my thanks to all the officials who kindly supplied me with information.

I am especially grateful to Miss Barbara Pellow, assistant at the *Centre Européen de l'Entreprise Public,* who has been kind enough to read my manuscript from a linguistic viewpoint. No blame should be cast upon her for my bad handling of the English language and existing errors in that respect are due to changes of mine subsequent to her reading.

Finally I am most grateful to the University of Uppsala for granting me a scholarship and for the financial assistance in printing my thesis. I also thank my professor, Mr Lars Hjerner, for his very useful support.

Stockholm in January 1976

Göran Lysén

Abbreviations

AJCL	American Journal of Comparative Law
BYIL	British Year Book of International Law
Cahiers	Cahiers de Droit Européen
CMLReview	Common Market Law Review
EAEC	European Atomic Energy Community
EC (=CE)	European Communities
ECSC	European Coal and Steel Community
EEC	European Economic Community
EGBGB	Einführungsgesetz zum Bürgerlichen Gesetzbuche
Euratom	European Atomic Energy Community
Haftung des Staates	Haftung des Staates für rechtswidriges Verhalten seiner Organe
IAEA	International Atomic Energy Agency
ICC	International Chamber of Commerce
ICJ	International Court of Justice
NJW	Neue Juristische Wochenschrift
O.J. (=J.O.)	Official Journal of the European Communities
R.V:2	Recueil de la Jurisprudence de la Cour de Justices des Communautés Européennes, volume five, page 2, French version, 1973 onwards R. 1973:2
TfR	Tidsskrift for Rettsvitenskap
The Court	The Court of Justice of the European Communities
ZaöRVR	Zeitschrift für ausländisches öffenliches Recht und Völkerrecht

Cases of the Court of Justice of the EC

14

R.XIII:469	Anne Collignon, épouse Jean-Claude Muller *v.* Commission des CE.
R.XIV:211	Firma Molkerei-Zentrale Westfalen/Lippe GmbH *v.* Hauptzollamt Paderborn (demande de décision préjudicielle).
R.XIV:431	Henri Labeyrie *v.* Commission des CE.
R.XIV:575	Claude Moise Sayag et S.A. Zürich *v.* Jean-Pierre Leduc, Denise Thonnon, épouse Leduc, et S.A. la Concorde (demande de décision préjudicielle).
R.XIV:661	Société par Actions Salgoil *v.* Ministère du Commerce Extérieur de la République Italienne (demande de décision préjudicielle).
R.XV:1	Walt Wilhelm et autres *v.* Bundeskartellamt (demande de décision préjudicielle).
R.XV:145	Jeannette Fux *v.* Commission des CE.
R.XV:211	Sociaal Fonds voor de Diamantarbeiders *v.* S.A. Ch. Brachfeld & Sons et Chougol Diamond Co. (demande de décision préjudicielle).
R.XV:329	Claude Sayag et S.A. Zürich *v.* Jean-Pierre Leduc, Denise Thonnon et S.A. la Concorde (demande de décision préjudicielle).
R.XV:419	Erich Stauder *v.* ville d'Ulm-Socialamt (demande de décision préjudicielle).
R.XVI:47	Commission des CE *v.* République Italienne.
R.XVI:325	Denise Riches-Parise et autres *v.* Commission des CE.
R.XVI:547	Anneliese Fiehn *v.* Commission des CE.
R.XVI:825	Franz Grad *v.* Finanzamt Traustein (demande de décision préjudicielle).
R.XVI:1125	Internationale Handelsgesellschaft mbH *v.* Einfuhr- und Vorratsstelle für Getreide und Futtermittel (demande de décision préjudicielle).
R.XVI:1213	Spa SACE *v.* Ministère des Finances de la République Italienne (demande de décision préjudicielle).
R.XVII:197	Società industriale metallurgica di Napoli (Simet) *v.* Commission des CE.
R.XVII:231	Commission des CE *v.* Conseil des CE.
R.XVII:263	Alfons Lütticke GmbH *v.* Commission des CE.
R.XVII:325	Aktien-Zuckerfabrik Schöppenstedt *v.* Conseil des CE.
R.XVII:975	Interfood GmbH *v.* Hauptzollamt Hamburg Ericus (demande de décision préjudicielle)
R.XVIII:391	Compagnie d'approvisionnement, de transport et de crédit SA et Grands Moulins de Paris SA *v.* Commission des CE.
R.XVIII:618	Imperial Chemical Industries Ltd. (ICI) *v.* Commission des CE.

Cases of national courts

France:

Blanco Case, Tribunal des Conflits, Recueil 1873, S61

Comptoir agricole des pay-bas normands *v.* ONIC, Conseil d'État, 4.2.1969, Recueil 1969, pp. 610—611

Cour d'Appel de Paris, Gazette du Palais 1973, nos 262—263 in Director-General of Customs *v.* Société des Cafés and others

Germany:

Internationale Handelsgesellschaft mbH *v.* Einfuhr- und Vorratsstelle für Getreide und Futtermittel (Case 2 BvL 52/71) before German Federal Constitutional Court, referred in NJW 1974, pp. 1697—1704, English translation in Common Market Law Reports 1974, Vol. 2, p. 540f.

Italy:

Italian Court of Appeal, Schiavello *v.* Nexi, referred in Giurisprudenza Italiana 1971 (1), pp. 1861—1868.

Belgium:

Tribunal de première instance de Bruxelles, 15/4 1966, Vanhove *v.* High Authority

Belgium Cour de Cassation 27/5/1971, État Belge *v.* SA Fromagerie Franco-Suiss Le Ski, Journal des Tribunaux 1971, p. 471.

Conseil d'État, 19.9.1972, Antwerp Meat Import *v.* État Belge, Recueil 1972, pp. 686—690.

Introduction

The European Communities stand for integration. The word *integer* originates from the Latin language and means *whole*. This is to say bringing the disparate parts of Europe together into one economic and political unit—at least in selected areas— which emerges from the aims of the Communities established in the preambles and declarations of principles in the international Treaties creating them, but this has also been expressed later on in elaborated reports and statements such as the Werner and Davignon reports. The Communities are furthermore a good example of *formal integration* since the procedure of integration is working within a well defined legal framework with institutions and other organs of the Communities involving a continuous cooperation and decision-making of the Member-States represented within the common organs. From this viewpoint the Communities belong to the long range of international organisations such as ECE, IMF, EFTA, OECD, EID, GATT etc. Integration can also take place *de facto* (no coordinated cooperation between states) as the world trade partly has done during the last hundred years, development being inter-rupted during the period between the two World Wars. The two kinds of integration do not work separately and independently from each other but there is an interplay between these two phenomena in promoting each other.

Different international organisations represent and may be related to various levels of integration and scope[1] where the level expresses the geographical extent (local, regional etc) whilst the scope indicates the extent of integration related to single projects, selected areas or total integration. Most international organisations could be arranged in such a way described; however, most of them have a rather limited scope of integration and they have because of that also limited powers. In the traditional international organisation all decisions are taken unanimously by the member-states of the organisation; note however the particular conditions prevailing for the international utility corporation. The specific means of integration given to the European Communities which will appear from Part 1, is comprehensive and far-reaching and separates these organisations from the traditional ones.

The speed of integration by an organisation is dependent on the political will of the members and the institutional framework of the organisation. Since the national interest of the Member-States, which are guarded by the national representatives, have to be moulded together to form a basis for

---

[1] Sundström, G O Zacharias, *The public international utility corporation*, p. 66.

decisions (often package-deals) within an international organisation, it is very important for the speed of integration and the strength of the organisation that the common interest of the organisation, which normally is also a primary interest of the members in the long run, is safeguarded by an independent body within the organisation. This is done by the Commission in the European Communities.

When an integration process has started to take place, it often leads to an increased acceleration of integration. This tends to necessitate a broadening of the areas for integration. This has happened to the GATT-conference which now, after having abolished most trade barriers of tariffs and quotas, has to tackle so-called technical barriers of trade in order to progress in liberating the world trade for which the conference however has not originally been constructed. When integration is extended to most fields of activites in society the integrated parts become increasingly more dependent on each other. This tends to provoke a further coordination but also an extension of the scope of the integration involving a substantial transfer of decision-making power to the organisation from the member-states. This stage can be said to have been achieved in the European Communities which is shown *inter alia* by the above-mentioned Davignon and Werner reports, but is also the crucial point in the integration process, since, if progress is not made, there is a risk that the organisation will desintegrate and descend to an organisation of more traditional features.

Attempts to unify Europe have been made several times in history, one may think of Charles the Great, Napoleon and Hitler but the integration process which was started by the "Six" (Belgium, France, Germany Holland, Italy and Luxembourg) after the second World War is indeed the first practical attempt to bring Europe together by peaceful means in order to avert any future war, bring the peoples of Europe closer together and improve their living-conditions. This integration process started by the signing of the European Coal and Steel Treaty in 1951 in Paris which came into force July 25, 1952. The integration of the coal and steel industries under the authority of a supranational body was mainly dictated by the wish to make it impossible for Germany or France alone to control these industries important for war preparation. The Coal and Steel Community was entrusted with the following institutions: the High Authority, the Assembly, the Council and the Court.

The failure of creating a European Army emphasised the despair and powerlessness of the former world powers after the war and initiated the "Six" to establishing the European Economic Community and the European Atomic Energy Community in order to promote economic growth and raise the standard of living, but here one should not forget political aims and considerations inherent in the economic field. These treaties were signed in Rome in 1957 and came into force January 1, 1958. Each of the two

Communities had the following institutions: an Assembly, a Council, a Commission and a Court. It seemed irrational to have so many institutions prescribed in the Treaties, therefore a third convention[2] was concluded in Rome which created a single parliamentary Assembly and a single Court of Justice common to all three Communities. These institutions act in accordance with the tasks and authorities laid down in the different Treaties. It should be pointed out that certain material differences exist especially between the Treaty of Paris and the two Treaties of Rome. Through the so-called Merger-Treaty[3] the Communities shared a single Council and a single Commission. The tasks and authorities of these institutions are determined by the rules laid down in the different Treaties and the Merger-Treaty. For a long time there have been plans to merge the three Treaties but this has not yet materialised due amongst other things, to disagreement concerning the competency of the institutions.

The EEC has undoubtedly the most far-reaching aims which are to be found in its articles 2 and 3. More specifically, one notes a customs union and a common agricultural policy both of which have materialised. Furthermore, the obstacles to the free movement of persons, services, goods and capital (the four liberties) shall be abolished and to that end the approximation of laws of the Member-States shall take place to the extent required for the proper functioning of the common market which indeed is an enormous task but substantial progress has been made in certain areas. For the free movement of goods and services the competition rules in particular in articles 85 and 86 are of great importance to prevent market-sharing and other measures for restricting trade in the Common Market i.e. creation of private trade barriers. In order to implement the objectives of the Treaty this necessitates sometimes far-going coordination of policies and restructual measures which is practically done by the Council and the Commission through legislating measures having affect in all the Member-States. It is not astonishing that the individuals of the Communities some-times will be victims of the integration process and suffer damage. Further-more, it is obvious that sometimes the interest of the individual person is opposed to the interest of integration—at least in the short run. Too much concern cannot be shown in this respect, since it otherwise would hamper the integration which is considered to have high priority and to be to the benefit of society in general by the Member-States.

[2] Convention relating to certain institutions common to the European Communities (see artt. 1 to 4) certain articles were thereby changed in the ECSC Treaty. The merger also concerned the Economic and Social Committee in the EEC and EAEC Treaties.

[3] Treaty establishing a Single Council and a Single Commission of the European Communities which came into force July 1, 1967 (see artt. 1 and 9) by which articles were abrogated or changed in all the Treaties.

Moreover, it appears from the Treaties that the individuals have few possibilities to directly influence or to contest measures purporting to new orders which they accordingly often have to abide by due to the institutional structure and legal order of the Treaties which in many respects differ from those of the Member-States. However, one should note that coal and steel undertakings and their associations as defined in the ECSC Treaty have a greater possibility to challenge legislative measures of the Commission which also involve policy questions than individuals according to the Rome Treaties. In this context of carrying out the Treaties the indemnity action becomes an important element giving compensation in certain situations to individuals but all inconveniences are not carrying a right to indemnity; furthermore, the Treaties and other texts making an integrated part of them do not give cause to reparation (*Continentale Case*, R. 1975:134). One can however say, that the balance between the necessity of the performance of the Treaties and the interests of the individuals to some extent is considered in the indemnity action as such.

The articles in the Rome Treaties dealing with the indemnity action have been given an ambiguous phrasing, neither has the action in the ECSC Treaty been given an exact formulation. The Court has here—as in many other fields of community law—been forced to elaborate this recourse through its case-law and has thereby also reinforced the protection which the indemnity action gives to the individuals for which the insufficient parliamentary control in the institutional framework has been an essential reason. How the indemnity action has been developed and formed under the Treaties is the aim of the coming description and will appear in detail. Since there are connections in serveral respects between non-contractual and contractual liability, the latter liability of the Communities has been included in the description.

The institutions and other organs of the Communities are presumed to perform their administrative work in a correct and efficient manner, and the legislating bodies must observe that issued acts are in conformity with the Treaties and other relevant community legislation but to those has been added by the Court general principles of law. This means for example that the community legislation also has to comply with fundamental rights where *inter alia* the European conventions of human rights may give guidance. One must in general conclude that the Court plays an active and very important role in the integration process. The Court's opinion many times indicates proper directions of development. Doubtless the Court is one of the most highly qualified courts of the world.

In 1969 in the Hague the Heads of State of the Member-States agreed to direct the integration process to development into an economic and monetary union. This *European Union* has been scheduled to 1980. However, it is unlikely that the Communities will achieve this aim by that date, since many obstacles and difficulties have come in their way such as Great Britain's so-called renegotiations, the oil crisis, the world wide recession, although some progress has been attained. In such a situation it is easy to become pessimistic regarding the credibility of a united Europe free from war and in a healthy and wealthy state which is indeed the very basis for an independent Europe being able to help the poor countries of the world. In this context it is essential not to loose the right proportions and to keep in mind how much progress already has been attained considering the very short time the Communities have existed, for example that today the possibility of a war in Western Europe is incredible, which many people take for granted and forget that the West European courtries have been fighting each other for more than one thousand years. The integration of Europe which does not mean a standardised way of living in its various parts, is a long term project involving enormous difficulties which cannot be overcome in a period of five or ten years, but the daily work of the community institutions with small practical progress creates the basis for further progress. Finally one should keep in mind, that the countries of Europe need to cooperate in order to be able to solve problems affecting all of them for survival, and this is also true for the rest of the world, but a good practice in cooperation is progress at the local and regional level.

Part one
Notes on the Legal Framework of the European Communities

Chapter one

The Institutions and some community organs

§ 1.1 The Council, the Commission, the Parliament, and the Court

The Council is the highest political organ within the Communities, which represents, on the one hand, the interests of the Member-States and, on the other, the interests of the Communities and its political will is decisive for the development of the Communities and of European integration. The Council is formed by representatives from each of the nine Member-States— normally one minister but more than one may be present. The Member-States are represented by their ministers of Foreign Affairs but also quite often by other ministers depending on the matters to be dealt with. The chairmanship of the Council rotates between the Member-States at six-monthly intervals in alphabetical order, beginning with Belgium for the first six months of 1973, followed by Denmark for the second half. The Council establishes its own internal regulations and working organisation as do the other institutions, and decides which organs are to assist it. The meetings of the Council are not public but members of the Commission are entitled to participate unless the Council decides otherwise.

The tasks and authorities of the Council vary according to the different Treaties; many of the tasks and authorities of the Council of the Treaties of Rome are conferred to the High Authority (Commission) according to the ECSC Treaty[1]. The tasks of that Council are to harmonise the measures of the Commission with the general economic policies of the governments of the Member-States[2]. The tasks and authorities of the Council according to the EAEC Treaty are evident from article 115 and the specific provisions in the Treaty and concerning the Council of the EEC Treaty, from article 145.

The Council has to make a great number of decisions according to the Treaties of Rome[3]. These are made by a simple majority of its members unless the Treaties provide otherwise. For certain decisions which in general entail more extensive engagements for the Member-States unanimity is required. Sometimes the Council has to act by qualified majority where the four larger states have ten votes each, Belgium and Holland five each, Ireland and Denmark three each, and Luxembourg two, which makes a total of 58 votes and means that 41 must be in favour of the adoption of a proposal from the Commission, and 41 votes must be in favour cast by at least six members in other cases. Owing to the rules of voting, the small Member-States are hereby ensured an important ascendancy in the Council, and the capacity of actions is not theoretically paralysed because of a veto by a Member-State. In practice, however, most of the decisions are made unanimously which doesn't mean that the rules of majority decisions lack significance but give pressure to reach a unanimous decision. Cf. the crisis in 1965/66 and the following so-called compromise of Luxembourg, with the main purpose to protect the essential interests of a Member-State[4].

In performing its tasks according to the Treaties of Rome the Council issues the following legal acts: regulations, directives, decisions, recommendations and opinions[5], by which the Council has to a certain extent the possibility to choose the type of act. The *regulations* are in all parts binding and directly applicable in every Member-State without an act of transformation into national law, i.e. they are directly applicable to the affected authorities and individuals. *Directives* are only binding upon the Member-State or States to which they are addressed and only express the aims to be achieved while the mode and means of implementation are left to be decided by the Member-States themselves; sometimes, however, the directives are worked out in great detail which does not leave much scope of action to the individual state. In principle, some kind of transformation act has to be made in the Member-States to change the directives into national law. *Decisions* are in all parts binding on anyone to whom they are addressed. Decisions which are addressed to individual moral or physical persons involving a pecuniary obligation are directly enforceable in accordance with the national rules in the Member-States at which the national authorities only have to examine the authenticity of the decision[6]. Finally, the Council gives *recommendations* and *opinions* which are not binding.

The decisions of the Council are prepared by a *Committee of Permanent Representatives* from the Member-States[7]. The Committee consists of the permanent representatives from the Member-States accredited to the Communities. Members of the Commission have the right to take part in the meetings of the Committee.

The Commission is[8] so to speak the real *European* institution and has supranational character and safeguards the interests of the Community. It is composed of thirteen members, two from the four larger countries and one from each of the others, who are appointed by the governments of the Member-States in mutual agreement which means that each government appoints its "own member". The members of the Commission have to fulfil their office in complete independence in favour of the interest of the Community and are not allowed to demand or receive instructions from governments, the Council or others.

The merged Commission consists of a General Secretariat, a legal Department, a statistical office, nineteen Directorates-General, and a small number of specialised services. Each member of the Commission is in charge of and responsible for one or more specialised departments. The Commission acts as one body and decisions are made by simple majority, only a limited amount of power is delegated to a single member and then only for strictly technical matters in accordance with the approach of the Commission.

The tasks of the Commission are laid down in the Treaties[9] and are mainly as follows[10]: the guardian of the Treaties, the executant and the initiator and driving force of community policies and the exponent of the interests of the Community to the Council. The Commission is entrusted with wide executive powers and may take the same legal acts as the Council in force of the Rome Treaties themselves and due to delegation of power by the Council (the High Authority has extensive rule making powers and issues decisions and recommendations and delivers opinions). Thus the Commission prepares the orders of implementation following from the Treaties or Council enactments, applies the provisions of the Treaties in particular cases, and administers different funds within the Treaties and within the EEC for exemple, the European Social Fund, the European Development Fund and the European Guidance and Guarantee Fund. Finally, the Commission may authorise derogations from certain obligations at the request of a Member-State. Moreover, the Commission conducts the commercial negotiations (art. 113, see also art. 228) with third countries assisted by a special committee within the framework of directives from the Council; note that the procedure concerning enlargement and association to the Communities mainly involves the Council.

The Parliamentary Assembly is composed of members from the national parliaments of the Member-States who are appointed according to the rules determined in each separate state. As a result of the enlargement the number of seats was increased from 142 to 198 where the larger countries hold 36 seats each, 14 each for Belgium and Holland, 10 each for Denmark and Ireland and 6 for Luxembourg. There are no national sections but only European level political groups.

The tasks and authorities of the Parliament are today small and consist of advisory and supervisory powers. The members of the Parliament may put written as well as oral questions both to the Commission and the Council. According to article 140(2) EEC Treaty the members of the Commission may attend all the meetings of the Parliament and at their request be heard on behalf of the Commission which implies answering oral and written questions put by the Parliament and its members; concerning the Council, see article 140 (4).

The Parliament has power in three fields: legislation, control of the activities of the Commission and budgetary matters. In the first field it has only advisory power[11]. Regarding the second, if a motion of censure is carried by a majority of two thirds of the votes cast, representing a majority of the members of the Parliament, the members of the Commission shall resign collectively[12].

By the Council decision of April 21, 1970 the Communities got their own financial resources to be set up succesively from January 1, 1971 till 1978. With the increased power and responsibilities of the Communities it was necessary at the same time to strengthen the budgetary powers of the Parliament (Treaty of April 22, 1970), which are related to the "free" part of the budget, giving the Parliament the final right of decision from 1975. In 1973 the Commission put forward a proposal to further strengthen the budgetary powers (*Bulletin of the EC,* supplement 9/73).

The Court of Justice. According to the Treaties of Rome[13] "The Court shall ensure the observance of law in the interpretation and application of this Treaty"; also, the ECSC Treaty contains a similar provision (art. 31). The Court, which has its residence in Luxembourg, shall consist of nine judges appointed by common accord with the governments of the Member-States for terms of six years. This number can be increased after a request by the Court and by a unanimous decision of the Council[14]. The Court may lay down its own procedure which requires the unanimous approval of the Council. The judges shall elect the President of the Court amongst themselves, he will conduct the work, control the Court and will be chairman in sessions as well as being responsible for the staff.

Most cases before the Court are decided in plenary sessions which in certain cases are provided for in the Treaties but decisions are also made by sections of the Court (three or five judges), and certain urgent matters are handled by the President alone. In each case a judge is called upon to be reporter.

The Court is assisted by four advocates-general of whom one is on duty in each case. They shall independently submit to the Court a summing-up of the case with a motivated conclusion.

§ 1.2 Some Community organs

The Economic and Social Committee (144 members) for the EEC and EAEC shall ensure that the most important interest groups in society may influence the decisions of the Council and the Commission and shall, according to a number of provisions in the Treaties, be consulted by these institutions before measures are taken and decisions made.

The Consultative Committee for the ECSC (81 members) has a function similar to the above-mentioned committee.

The Committee of Permanent Representatives (CORPER) see § 1.1.

The European Social Fund has the task of supporting the possibilities of employment of manpower and its geographical and professional mobility in the Community.

European Development Fund gives aid to overseas countries and other territories associated with the EEC.

The European Investment Bank (articles 129 and 130 of the EEC Treaty), having its own legal personality, shall contribute to a balanced and harmonious development of the Common Market which *inter alia* means support to undeveloped regions of the Market and to the modernisation of industries.

European Agricultural Guidance and Guarantee Fund supports the market (prices) and improves structures.

The Regional Development Fund.

The European Monetary Fund endowed with legal personality is the embryo in a monetary organisation of the EEC.

Atomic Supply Agency (art. 54 (1) EAEC Treaty).

There are a lot of committees such as the ones of Governors of Central Banks, Economic Policy, Special Agriculture, Budgetary Policy, Conjunctual Policy, Monetary, Permanent Committee of Employment, etc. which are connected with the Council; also the Commission has established a number of advisory committees.

The Management Committees are a special group of committees which from the beginning were only concerned with agricultural marketing but nowadays have become involved in other fields. If the Commission is going to enact in force of delegated power from the Council the draft proposal is sent to the committee concerned which gives an opinion resulting from the same way of voting as in the Council where the opinion is not binding upon the Commission; but if the opinion has been given by a qualified majority and the Commission takes another view in its decision, contrary to the opinion of the committee, the matter will pend before the Council which must reserve it within one month. When the Commission's decision is in line with the opinion of the committee, or the opinion has not been taken by a qualified majority, there will be no appeal to the Council.

Footnotes chapter one

1. See artt. 14 and 15 of the Treaty. The powers of the High Authority are in certain respects more far-reaching and modelled differently than those of the Commission based on the Treaties of Rome.

2. Art. 26 (1) of the ECSC Treaty.

3. See art. 28 concerning the rules of voting in the ECSC Treaty; artt. 148 and 118 of the EEC and EAEC Treaties.

4. In the EEC the Council has increasingly become the centre of power and according to *Rapport Vedel* (*Bulletin of the EC,* p. 25f suppl. 4/72) there is a growing imbalance between the institutions in favour of the Council which has weakened the political function of the Commission, especially the practice of unanimous voting deprives the Commission of its right in article 149 and the legal force of its proposals. However, there are recent attempts to reintroduce the majority voting.

5. Art. 189 of the EEC Treaty, and art. 161 of the EAEC Treaty.

6. Art. 192 of the EEC Treaty and art. 164 of the EAEC Treaty; see also art. 92 of the ECSC Treaty.

7. Art. 4 of the Merger-Treaty.

8. See artt. 9—19 of the Merger-Treaty.

9. Artt. 155 of the EEC Treaty, 124 EAEC Treaty and 8 and 14 of the ECSC Treaty.

10. See e.g. *How the European Community's institutions work* by Emile Noel, 1973 and *La Communauté Européenne, aujourd'hui, demain,* Bureau of information of the EC, Paris 1973.

11. See art. 137.

12. Art. 144.

13. Art. 164 of the EEC Treaty and art. 136 of the EAEC Treaty.

14. It should be noted, that the Treaties do not contain any provision concerning the nationality of the judges; theoretically it would be possible to have nine judges from one country but each country has its "own" judge.

Chapter two

The Court of Justice

§ 2.1 The Competence

The Court has no general competence to handle cases concerning the interpretation and application of community law but its competence is based on explicit provisions in the Treaties. Furthermore, the cases in which a Community is a party, shall not be excluded from the jurisdictions of national courts unless the Court has been given competency. Through the possibility of giving preliminary rulings (*à titre préjudiciel*) the Court[1] has been ensured ascendancy concerning the interpretation of community law over the national courts. The decision of the Court is binding upon the national court, but it is up to the latter, in the concrete case, to put the interpreted rules into practice.

The Court has, however, extensive jurisdiction and can be said to function as an international court, a constitutional and administrative court and a civil and criminal court.

International court. An action may be brought against a Member-State and the description shows (1) the competence (2) those entitled to bring an action before the Court (3) the cause:

EEC	(1) the articles 169, 170 and 180
Treaty	(2) the Commission (art. 169), a State (art. 170) and the Board of Directors of the European Investment Bank (art. 180 a)
	(3) failure to fulfil the obligations of the Treaty or of the Statutes of the European Investment Bank
EAEC	(1) the articles 141, 142 and 143
Treaty	(2) the Commission (art. 141) and a State (art. 141)
	(3) failure to fulfil the obligations of the Treaty
ECSC	(1) the article 89 (1)
Treaty	(2) a State (art. 89 (1)
	(3) disputes between MemberStates concerning the application of the Treaty

With the exclusion of every other court the Member-States, according to the Treaties, must let the Court settle disputes concerning the interpretation and application of the Treaties[2] even if e.g. the ICJ of the Hague would also be competent. Through a prorogation-clause[3] the Court shall be competent to give a judgement on any dispute between the Member-States connected with the subjects of the Treaties. If the Court finds a measure incompatible with a Treaty, a judgement will result in a confirmation thereof, since there are no remedies for sanctions; note however, the special authorities of the High Authority according to the ECSC Treaty article 88 (3); the Member-States of the Treaties of Rome are bound to take the measures required for the implementation of the judgement of the Court.

Constitutional and Administrative Court. An action concerning the legality of an act can be brought against the Council or the Commission. This is a legal control of the legislative and administrative measures of these institutions (regulations, directives, decisions and acts sui generis). Acts (decisions and recommendations) of the High Authority (Commission) may also be challenged:

	EEC^4	EAEC	ECSC
Competence (articles)	173	146	33
Grounds of the action	lack of competence, infringement of an essential procedural requirement, infringement of the Treaty or any rule of law relating to its application, or misuse of powers		same as the Rome Treaties
Persons entitled to an action	Member-States, the Council, the Commission, and natural and legal persons concerning decisions addressed to them and decisions in the form of decisions to others or regulations, if they directly and individually concern them		Member-States, the Council, and undertakings or associations of undertakings (art. 48 and 80) including both decisions and recommendations concerning them individually and general decisions and recommendations involving misuse of powers affecting them

The Court may, according to the ECSC Treaty (art. 38), upon application by a Member-State or the High Authority, declare an act of the Parliament or of the Council to be void on grounds of lack of competency, or infringement of an essential procedural requirement.

The action of annulment shall be brought before the Court within a certain period of time, and if the Court recognises the act as illegal, it will abrogate the contested measure (*cassation*). The institution whose measure is declared null and void has to take the necessary steps to implement the judgement of the Court[5].

If the Council of the Rome Treaties or the Commission, in violation of the Treaties, should fail to act and if they haven't acted within a certain period of time though called to do so, the matter may be referred to the Court:

	EEC	EAEC	ECSC
Competence (articles)	175	148	35 (not identical to the provisions of the Rome Treaties)
Entitled to an action	Member-States, all institutions, and natural and legal persons, if an institution has failed to address to that person any act[6] other than recommendations and opinions		Member-States, the Council, and undertakings and associations of them[7]

Through *l'exception d'illégalité* a legal protection has been created for everyone against illegal regulations (decisions and recommendations of the ECSC Treaty) even though the stipulated period for an action for annulment is ended. These provisions (artt. 184 of the EEC Treaty, 156 of the EAEC Treaty and 36 (3) of the ECSC Treaty) are of great importance to individuals who cannot challenge regulations in general. They have the possibility to invoke that a regulation in accordance with the grounds for an action of annulment is not applicable in a concrete case. If the Court finds the objection well founded the regulation is not declared null and void but is found to be inapplicable in that case.

Civil and Criminal Court. The Court is, in accordance with the articles 178 and 151 of the Rome Treaties, competent to settle disputes concerning non-contractual liability provided for in articles 215 and 188 of the above mentioned Treaties. The Court is also competent according to articles 34 and 40 of the ECSC Treaty to settle disputes concerning non-contractual liability. Both States and individual persons may bring such a case before the Court; actions for these claims must be lodged within a period of five years after the event causing the damage.

The Court is also competent[8] to give a decision pursuant to a *clause compromissoire* (i.e. a prorogation clause) contained in a contract concluded by or on behalf of a Community which excludes *inter alia* national courts from having competency.

Furthermore, the Court is competent to handle disputes between the Communities and their servants according to article 179 of the EEC Treaty, 152 of the EAEC Treaty and 42 of the ECSC Treaty[9].

According to articles 172 of the EEC, 144 of the EAEC and 36 of the ECSC Treaties, these articles provide conditions for the Court to exercise unlimited jurisdiction (*une compétence de pleine juridiction*) with regard to imposed penalties.

§ 2.2 The Procedure

The procedure before the Court is provided for in the Treaties, in separate protocols concerning the Statutes of the Court (Statutes), in Rules of Procedure (R.P.), Additional R.P. and in instruction to the Registrar. The procedure is divided into two stages: one written and one oral[10] and is in its nature contradictory, accusatorial and inquisitorial. The proceedings before the Court are public unless the Court decides otherwise which may only be done for substantial reasons. In each case one of the official languages is used as the procedural language, hereby the principal rule is that the plaintiff chooses the language; nevertheless, there are three exceptions (see art. 29 of R.P.). According to the Rules of Procedure the process is composed of an ordinary one and a special one of which the coming description will mainly be devoted to the ordinary one.

The written procedure
A case is brought before the Court by a formal request addressed to the Registrar in accordance[11] with what is stipulated in articles 37 and 38 of the Rules of Procedure from which it *inter alia* appears that the request shall contain the name and the domicile of the plaintiff, the name of the party against whom the action is lodged, the subject of the dispute, conclusions, a short summary of the main arguments on which the action is based and means of proof available where appropriate. Concerning preliminary rulings the proceedings are instituted by a decision of the national court of which the Registrar is notified[12]. The request is communicated to the defendant who has to produce a statement of defence[13] whereupon may follow a reply and a further reply. On the basis of that material the reporting judge elaborates a summing-up of the case (*rapport préalable*) which is presented before a section of the Court (not public) whereupon the Court considers what measures are suitable for calling up evidence (art. 45 of the R.P.) such as 1) the personal appearance of the parties 2) a request for information and production of documents 3) evidence by witnesses 4) expert examination and report and 5) inspection *in situ*. After the proper measures have been ordered and carried out, the reporting judge elaborates his *rapport audience* which contains the facts of the case, the claims and adductions of the parties.

The oral procedure
This part begins with the presentation of the reporting judge's *rapport audience* after which follows the hearings of witnesses and experts[14], the conclusions of the parties which must be presented by legal advisers and representatives[15], additional questions by the judges and the Advocate-General to the parties and finally, the submissions of the Advocate-General which are generally delivered in a later public seance.

After the oral and public part, the deliberations of the Court commence which are not public and in which only judges who have participated in the oral part have a right to participate (art. 27 (2) of the R.P.). During the deliberations of the Court each judge has to express and motivate his opinion in the case; the voting is done by simple majority. The judgement appears as a common work of the Court and subsequently dissenting votes are not included. The judgement has the formal similarity of a French one but is in reality more similar to a German one, the former appearing as a conclusion and the latter as a discussion with the parties. The judgement is delivered in open court and comes immediately into force (art. 65 of the R.P.).

A request for intervention[16] for supporting a party must be made to the Court before the oral part of the proceedings; the institutions and Member-States do not have to show a justifiable interest in the result of the case, whereas for individuals there are certain restrictions.

The Court shall give a ruling on the court costs[17]; the winning party has the right to be paid for his costs upon which the Court may use its discretion; see further the rules in articles 69—75 of the R.P. If one party finds that he is unable to face the costs he may apply for the benefit of free legal aid which is decided on by a section of the Court with regard to the grounds of the proceedings already began or projected (art. 76 of the R.P. and artt. 4 and 5 of the Additional R.P.).

According to article 66 of the Rules of Procedure a judgement may, within a certain period from its deliverance at the request of a party or by the Court *ex officio,* be corrected insofar as clerical errors, and mistakes in reckoning or evident inaccuracies are concerned.

A judgement may also be changed by exceptional means[18] (artt. 97—100 of the R.P.) through an action by a third party for retrial or by revision (see e.g. *Jamet Case,* R. 1973:295 and *Serio Case,* R. 1974:671) by the Court of its own judgement. On a special request by a former party[19] the Court may interpret a judgement of its own with regard to its meanings and scope (see *Getreidehandel mbH Case,* R. 1973:1599).

The execution of a judgement of the Court[20] varies according to the matter of the case and the parties; for individuals it is provided in the Treaties that obligations to pay are executed by the national authorities in the Member-States who only have to examine the authenticity of the judgement.

Footnotes chapter two

1. *Interlocutory judgement* is a better expression than preliminary ruling, but the latter will be used, since it is employed in the English version of the EEC Treaty. By Council decision of November 26, 1974 article 165 of the EEC Treaty and corresponding articles of the other two Treaties were adjusted to enable the Court to refer to its chambers questions for preliminary rulings on certain conditions.

2. Art. 219 of the EEC Treaty, art. 193 of the EAEC Treaty and art. 87 of the ECSC Treaty.

3. Artt. 182 of the EEC Treaty, 154 of the EAEC Treaty and art. 89 (2) of the ECSC Treaty.

4. Decisions by the Board of Governors of the European Investment Bank may be challenged in the same way by Member-States, the Commission or by the Board of Directors (art. 180 b). Decisions of the Board of Directors may also be challenged in the same way by Member-States or the Commission in certain defined cases (art. 180 c).

5. Note what is provided for about non-contractual liability in art. 176 (2) of the EEC Treaty, art. 149 (2) of the EAEC Treaty and art. 34 of the ECSC Treaty.

6. ”any act” probably means a decision in a technical meaning. Concerning the admissibility to this action of individual persons the conditions are the same as in article 173 (2). Moreover, this article has not the same meaning as article 35 of the ECSC Treaty, and ”not defined position” probably implies the absence of any formal decision (absence in *stricti sensu*). See, *Le controle de la légalité des actes étatiques par la Cour de Justice des CE* by G Ferrière, p. 95 f.

7. In the case *Groupement des Industries Sidérurgiques Luxembourgeoises versus the High Authority* (R.II:53) the Court expressed (p. 85):
”le recours formé par le requérant en application troisième alinéa de l’article 35 du Traité est . . . un recours en annulation . . . tel que prévu à l’article 33 du Traité et dès lors soumis à ses conditions”.

8. Art. 181 of the EEC Treaty, art. 153 of the EAEC Treaty and art. 42 of the ECSC Treaty.

9. Discussions are carried on in order to create a court of first instance for disputes involving the staff and the institutions.

10. Statutes: EEC and EAEC art. 18 and ECSC art. 21.

11. See also the Statutes: EEC and EAEC art. 19 and ECSC art. 22.

12. Statutes: EEC art. 20, EAEC art. 21 and concerning ECSC art. 103 (2) of the R.P.

13. See art. 40 of the R.P. — About judgement by default of the defending party, see art. 94 of the R.P. and Statutes: EEC art. 38, EAEC art. 39 and ECSC art. 35. The Court may give such a judgement against which appeal may be made for a retrial.

14. Evidence may accordingly be brought before the Court during the preparation as well as during the trial.

15. See the Statutes: EEC and EAEC art. 17 and ECSC art. 20.

16. Statutes: EEC art. 37, EAEC art. 38 and ECSC art. 34. See also art. 93 of the R.P.

17. The proceedings are free of charge but a party has to pay the costs unnecessarily caused by him.

18. For the grounds see the Statutes: EEC artt. 39 and 41, EAEC artt. 40 and 42, and ECSC artt. 36 and 38.

19. Art. 102 of the R.P., Statutes: EEC art. 40, EAEC art. 41 and ECSC art. 37.

20. EEC artt. 187 and 192, EAEC artt. 153 and 164 and ECSC artt. 44 and 92.

Chapter three

The sources of community law

The Court has several times expressed the opinion that it and the other community institutions are only competent to interpret and apply community law[1]. A general definition of what community law is shall not be given here, but it is sufficient to note that (besides the Treaties) the law unilaterally emanating from the community institutions is community law.

The sources of law have in the description been arranged in accordance with their range and importance. They may be divided into two groups, namely first hand and supplementary sources. To the first category belong the texts of the Treaties together with them annexes and protocols (primary sources), and thereafter follow enactments by the Council and the Commission (secondary sources) which may be ranged among themselves. In addition to these is a third kind of source, namely the case-law of the Court. The supplementary sources consist of the national laws of the Member-States and rules in public international law. Hereto the Court is certainly observant of the case-law of the Member-States concerning the interpretation of community law and, finally, the judicial doctrine.

§ 3.1 The Treaties

The legal character of the Communities is difficult to define, and there is discord among the experts in public international law on whether the Communities should be regarded as a complex of agreements in the fields of public international law, an international organisation, a kind of union or a federation etc.[2]. If the Communities must be labelled, they certainly must be characterised as something much more than traditional treaties of public international law[3]. The developing community law constitutes its own, firm and original legal system[4]. W. Lorenz[5] expresses the opinion that the Treaties of the Communities are threefold in their nature including a) international conventions in the traditional sense b) constitutions and c) codifications, containing administrative law as well as private law. It is obvious that since the Communities are new creations, they cannot be arranged according to traditional public law, though they may in certain aspects be resolved into traditional terms.

They should also be a dynamic and flexible instrument in a world of expanding economy and trade and must be able to face these changes (note the EEC Treaty is talking about an economic community which is much more far-reaching than a common market). The Advocate-General Lagrange[6] expressed the following opinion concerning the nature of the ECSC Treaty:

"Enfin, la méthode d'interprétation stricte ainsi défendue serait celle qui doit toujours prévaloir lorsqu'il s'agit de traités internationaux, suivant les usages des juridictions internationales, telles que la Cour de la Haye. . . On pourrait sans doute rappeler que notre Cour n'est pas une juridiction internationale, mais la juridiction d'une Communauté créée par six États sur un type qui s'apparente beaucoup plus à une organisation fédérale qu'à une organisation internationale, et que le Traité dont la Court a pour mission d'assurer l'application, s'il a bien été conclu dans la forme des traités internationaux, et s'il en est un incontestablement, n'en constitue pas moin, du point de vue matériel, la charte de la Communauté, les règles de droit qui s'en dégagent constituant *le droit interne de cette Communauté*".

However, it should be kept in mind that the Communities consist of three treaties and that there are important differences between them. The ECSC Treaty contains a detailed programme of the objectives to be attained for which the High Autority has been endowed with a great amount of power of implementation, and which are related to a restricted sphere of the economies of the Member-States. Also, the EAEC Treaty contains a lot of detailed rules in a specific field, and consequently these Treaties do not give the institutions that much scope for supplementing and developing the Treaties. The EEC Treaty is different from these two others, as it practically affects the whole economic life of the Member-States and has the form of a frame treaty (*traité-cadre*).

The measures for the implementation of the objectives laid down in the Treaty have to a great extent been entrusted to the institutions and a great effort has been made to elaborate the division of competence between the institutions (see further § 3.2). The Community has furthermore been endowed with the dynamism and flexibility which makes it possible for it to adopt the measures required for the changing conditions in society (see art. 235).

The Treaties may be said to consist of institutional rules (see Chapter one), on the one hand, and on the other hand, material rules; the latter express the basic facts concerning the aims to be attained. These material rules may be divided into declarations (typical of the EEC Treaty) and self executing, constituting immediately existing law in the Member-States. These are so detailed and concrete that they at once create rights and liabilities for authorities and individuals who are affected by the rules. It is not always clear which are these rules, but the Court has, however, in some cases declared that certain rules which formally only bind the Member-

States also must have internal effects. In these cases the rules have implied clear and inevitable obligations for the Member-States which have not been left any choice of decision[7].

§ 3.2 The Law-making process

A summary of the tasks and authorities of the institutions is given under paragraph 1.1 from which it is clear *inter alia* that the Council and the Commission are responsible for the law-making activities within the Communities. Here follows a concise description[8] of the law-making processes including the form and publishing provisions which the Council and the Commission have to observe.

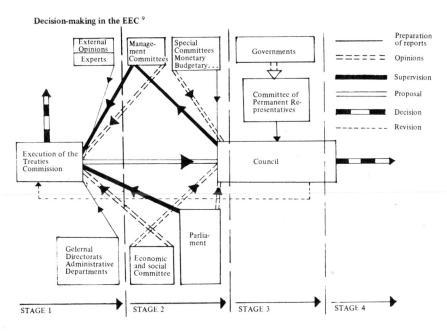

Decision-making in the EEC [9]

STAGE 1   STAGE 2   STAGE 3   STAGE 4

First stage. The Commission has almost the sole right to initiate proposals to be decided upon by the Council and is here a preparatory organ in relation to the Council which may only by a unanimous decision change or adopt amendments to a proposal from the Commission (art. 149 (1)), and a majority decision may only be taken if it is in conformity with the proposal from the Commission. However, the Council is entitled to request the Commission to undertake any study which the Council finds necessary in order to attain the common objectives and to submit appropriate proposals (art. 152).

During the elaboration of a proposal e.g. a regulation, the Commision consults national experts, top civil servants in the Member-States, political circles, different organisations on a community-european level and the Economic and Social Committee provided for in the Treaty (art. 198 (1)); the Commission has also close contacts with the Parliament. The Commission has extensively used its facultative right to consult the Committee. The Commission works out its final proposal within its own departments, which is adopted by the Members of the Commission by a majority vote where the minority abides by the majority decision; however, many decisions are, in fact, unanimous.

Second stage. After the Commission has submitted its proposal, the Council consults different committes and bodies. The most important committee is that of the Permanent Representatives of the Member-States which prepares the future work and gives authority to competent groups to carry out studies in depth. In this process the Commission is represented at all conferences and at all levels. The Parliament and the Economic and Social Committee shall according to a number of provisions be heard by the Council, and in a number of cases these bodies are consulted on the proper initiative of the Council.

Third stage. When the Committee of the Permanent Representatives is in agreement and the Commission has no objections there is no further discussion in the Council which decides on such matters *en bloc* as "point A", since the decisions of the Council can only be made by its members. On other matters a dialogue takes place between the Council and the Commission, which may alter its original proposal as long as the Council has not yet made a decision on the matter (art. 149 (2)). This means that the Commission is able to redraft a proposal after the Parliament and the Economic and Social Committee have delivered their opinions and take account of their views. A continued dialogue, however, may mean that the final version is removed from the redrafted one, therefore, the Commission has suggested[10] a "second reading" in the procedure concerning important rule making decisions of general application.

As mentioned in § 1.1. the Council has increasingly become the centre of power in the EEC and as a result of the unanimous voting in the Council, the Commission has largely concentrated on and looked towards the Council in trying to find out the political atmosphere for its proposals which has deminished the importance of other community bodies. Furthermore, many important decisions concerning European integration have been made in meetings[11] called *Sommet* meetings, where the rules of the majority decisions are inapplicable giving a predominance to larger countries. Therefore, in order to restore the balance laid down in the Treaty, the small countries would favour, on various levels, increased power of the Commission and the Parliament. The Council and to some degree also the Permanent Representatives are at a bottleneck in the decision making system, since they have a, tendency to pay too much attention to what sometimes seem to.be ridiculously small details, and there are discussions to let other community bodies take care of these details in order to ease the burden and to speed up the decison making procedure in the Council.

Fourth stage. When the Council has finally made a regulation, directive or a decision it shall state the reasons on which it is based and indicate references to any proposals and opinions which according to the Treaty were compulsory (art. 190). However, references are normally made to other received proposals and opinions; and in this context one shall not forget to read the preamble which gives the background and the explanatory notes.

Regulations shall be published in the *Official Journal* (Part L) of the Community (article 191 (1)) which is printed in all the official languages, and come into force the day which is provided for in the regulation, or otherwise on the twentieth day after publication. Directives and decisions shall be notified to those to whom they are addressed and come into force through the notification. In addition to the individual notification, directives and decisions are often published for the purpose of information. Concerning recommendations and opinions there are no specific rules in the Treaty, but they are often published in Part C of the Official Journal.

§ 3.3 The case law of the Court

Through the activities of the Court the Treaties and other community acts are interpreted and applied. In certain cases this involves an active creation of law (see Chapter nine). The decisions of the Court are only judicially binding in the concrete case but possess *une valeur d'orientation*[12]; although the Court has no obligation to follow its own precedents, this is, however, in practice normally done. In the preliminary ruling of the *Costa en Schaake Case* (R.IX:78) the Court expressed "il n'y a pas lieu à nouvelle interprétation de l'article 12 du traité CEE", when the matter of interpretation was identical with the one made in an earlier decision (*Van Gend & Loos Case,* R.IX:1) and did not contain any new element. Although the Court may review its own precedents, it seems necessary nevertheless in certain instances, if the Court has interpreted a treaty or an act issued by the Council or the Commission in a certain way, to change the treaty or the act to abrogate the interpretation adopted by the Court.

§ 3.4 National laws of Member-States

The Court has explicitly stated (*Uitdenbogerd Case,* R.VIII:101) that the community law and the national laws of the Member-States are two different and distinct legal systems. However, the community law is not comprehensive, and it must therefore be interpreted and supplemented. Since the Court cannot work in a vacuum it became natural to look to legal principles common to the national laws of the Member-States which because of historical facts are comparatively similar (concerns the "Six") even though there are no general and explicit references in the Treaties (note art. 33 of the ECSC Treaty and art. 173 of the EEC Treaty respectively "infringement of any rule of law relating to its application"). In the Treaties of Rome, however, a reference is made concerning the non-contractual liability of these Communities to "principes généraux communs aux droits des États membres" (articles 215 (2) and 188 (2) of the EEC and the EAEC Treaties respectively). Though there is no explicit provision at all in the ECSC Treaty the Court has nevertheless referred to these common principles:

"... pour la solution duquel le Traité ne contient pas de règles. La Cour, sous peine de commettre un déni de justice, est donc obligée de le résoudre en s'inspirant des règles reconnues par les législations, la doctrine et la jurisprudence des pays membres. Une étude de droit comparé fait ressortir que. . ."[13]

and in another case:

"...selon le droit de tous les États membres[14].

Advocate Lagrange[15] expresses the matter as follows:

"...il ne s'agit pas ici d'appliquer le droit italien ni le droit francais ni celui de tout autre pays de la Communauté, mais le droit du Traité, et c'est uniquement pour parvenir à l'élaboration de ce droit du Traité que l'étude des solutions juridiques nationales doivent etre entreprise, chaque fois qu'elle apparait nécessaire à cette fin".

It is an obvious fact that the Court by means of legal principles in the laws of the Member-States interprets and creates community law; a good example is the interpretation of the terms *Ermessenmissbrauch* and *détournement de pouvoir* which have been given a community law signification (see further Chapter nine).

Although the Court is not competent to apply national laws, in certain situations the Court is compelled to apply such laws at least in deciding preliminary matters in a case e.g. whether a party before the Court is a natural or legal person[16].

By means of law-approximation a common legal basis is created for the Member-States, which shall be done to the extent required for the proper functioning of the common market (art. 3 (h) EEC). In this context one should note article 235 which is a general clause by which the Member-States have delegated to the Community all the necessary power to undertake measures for the implementation of the aims laid down in the Treaty. The aims may however be interpreted restrictively or extensively depending on the present political situation.

The European Monetary Cooperation Fund was formed on the basis of article 235.

The general basis for approximations of laws is, however, article 100 in which it is provided that the Council shall, acting unanimously on a proposal from the Commission, issue directives for the approximation of such provisions laid down by law, regulations or administrative action in Member-States as directly affect the establishment or functioning of the common market. The directives are only binding upon the Member-States, and some kind of transformation into national legislation is necessary by which the forms and methods are left to the individual state to comply with the aims laid down in the directive. The forms in the different states may differ but the result shall remain the same. Sometimes it is more suitable to use a regulation and then article 235 may be the basis for such a measure as for example the proposed "European Company". There are also specific provisions concerning certain fields of activities for which approximation is explicitly provided, for example art. 27, customs matters, art. 57, right of establishment, art. 75, transport, art. 99, taxes. Finally, article 220 provides for concludings of international conventions between the Member-States.

Finally, mention should be made of the conflict between the community law and the national laws of the Member-States which may arise when incompatible rules contemporaneously contend for applicability. This problem belongs principally to the national courts which have to decide which law must be overruled, as neither the Court nor the other community institutions have the right to declare national law null and void. The intensity of the conflict differs according to the nature of the laws involved and their chronology. Owing to article 177 of the EEC Treaty the Court has had the opportunity to give its view of the relationship between the community law and the national laws of the Member-States by which the Court with great emphasis has upheld the priority of the former over the latter. It suffices here to quote the views expressed by the Court in the famous case of *Flamino Costa versus E.N.E.L.* (R.X:1158f) from 1964:

". . . attendu que la prééminence du droit communautaire est confirmée par l'article 189 aux termes duquel les règlements ont valeur 'obligatoire' et sont 'directement applicables dans tout État membre'; . . .que le transfert opéré par les États, de leur ordre juridique interne au profit de l'ordre juridique communautaire, des droits et obligations correspondant aux dispositions du traité, entraine donc une limitation définitive de leurs droits souverains contre laquelle ne saurait prévaloir un acte unilatéral ultérieur incompatible avec la notion de Communauté; . . ."

It is now evident that the national courts have been influenced by the Court's opinion since they seek by means of different interpretations to give priority to community law. In all the Member-States there seems to prevail a growing awareness that the community law should get the same force of influence in all the States which can only be done if community law is given priority[17]. If national law must stand aside it doen't mean that it is void, but only that it is not to be applied in the concrete case.

§ 3.5 Public international law

The legal subjects in the traditional international law were from the outset sovereign states, and later on i.a. international organisations[18], created by the states, were also added. The obligations that public international law imposes on the states are in general not exact, and many remedies which exist in municipal law are missing. In many fields there are no material rules at all, therefore, concerning the international organisations they have, in many cases, to resort to municipal law[19]. According to article 38 of the Statute of the International Court of Justice the sources of international law are:

1) International conventions, whether general or particular, establishing rules expressly recognized by the contesting States;
2) International custom, as evidence of a general practice accepted as law;
3) The general principles of law recognized by civilized nations;
4) Subject to the provisions of article 59[20], judicial decisions and the teachings of the most highly qualified publicists of the various nations, as subsidiary means for determination of rules of law.

The Court has indeed been more inclined to look for solutions in the laws of the Member-States than to public international law which certainly *inter alia* is a result of the non-comprehensibility of the latter. Although the Court would look to international law when it exercises its function as an international court the special character of the Treaties is ubiquitous and will affect the result. Furthermore, in a few cases the Court dealt with the relationship between GATT and community law. Following from the wording in article 173 of the EEC Treaty, it seems to involve the possible challenge before the Court of an international treaty concluded by the Council on behalf of the Community. However, the Council, the Commission or Member-States may obtain a preliminary ruling as to what extent an intended treaty is compatible or not with the provisions of the EEC Treaty (art. 228).

Footnotes chapter three

1. The Court has thus *inter alia* expressed in the *Storck Case,* R.V:63:
"... en vertu de l'article 8 du traité, la Haute Autorité n'est appelée à appliquer que le droit de
la Communauté; qu'elle n'est pas compétente pour appliquer le droit interne des États
membres; que, de meme, selon l'article 31 du traité, la Cour n'a qu'à assurer le respect du droit
dans l'interprétation et l'application du traité et des règlements d'exécution; qu'en règle générale, elle n'a pas à se prononcer sur les régles de droit interne",

and in the *Comptoir de Vente du Charbon de la Ruhr,* R.VI:890:
"... que dès lors la Cour ne peut ni interpréter, ni appliquer l'article 14 de la loi fondamentale
allemande dans l'examen de la légalité d'une décision de la Haute Autorite".

Moreover, note the *Casagrande Case,* R.1974:778:
"... dans le cadre de la procédure de l'article 177, la Cour ne peut se prononcer sur l'interprétation ou la validité de dispositions législatives de nature nationale, elle est cependant compétente
pour interpréter l'article 12 du règlement no 1612/68 et pour dire si cet article vise ou non
l'application de mesures d'encouragement telles que la mesure litigieuse".

When the Court gives a preliminary ruling, it certainly is incumbent on the Court to
make an interpretation, but if that interpretation is to have any practical value, it must
have a certain connection with the facts in the case, therefore the decision of the
national court is often given after the Court's interpretation.

2. W Friedmann, *The changing structure of international law,* p. 98 considers the
community treaties to stop short of the establishment of a federation.

3. See *Van Gend & Loos Case*, R.IX:23:
"attendu que l'objectif du traité C.E.E. qui est d'instituer un marché commun dont le fonctionnement concerne directement les justiciables de la Communauté, implique que ce traité constitue plus qu'un accord qui ne créerait que des obligations mutuelles entre les États contractants
... qu'il faut conclure de cet état de choses que la Communauté constitue un nouvel ordre
juridique de droit international, au profit duquel les États ont limité, bien que dans des domaines
restreints, leurs droits souverains, et dont les sujets sont non seulement les États membres mais
également leurs ressortissants".

4. See L Constantinesco, in *Revue trim. de Droit Européen 1966,* pp. 1—30.

5. *AJCL 1964,* p. 5.

6. *Fédération Charbonnière de Belgique Case,* R.II:263.

7. Concerning the EEC Treaty e.g. *Van Gend & Loos Case,* R.IX:1, *Costa Case,*
R.X:1141, *Lütticke Case,* R.XII:293, and *Molkerei Westfalen Case,* R.XIV:211.

8. The description is mainly related to the procedure of the Treaties of Rome and
references are made to articles in the EEC Treaty. According to the ECSC Treaty the
High Authority (Commission) issues decisions and recommendations and gives
opinions by itself or after consulting other institutions or organs, and in many cases
an approval by the Council is required concerning a measure to be taken by the
Commission (*avis conforme*) which in reality implies that the Council has the possibility to slow down or accelerate the speed of integration.

9. The present institutional and administrative position in the EEC under the direction of K Grdic et al. *Eurocooperation nr 3/4 1973.*

10. See document *COM (73) 570 final* of April 19, 1973 sect. IV-B-1.

11. Outside of the Treaties at special conferences with representatives from the
governments of the Member-States, decisions and agreements are made which are
nonetheless foreseen in the Treaties e.g. in article 167 (1) of the EEC Treaty

("common accord of the governments of the Member States"). Functionally, these improper decisions by the Council are connected with the community law and are of importance to the Court but will probably fall under the rules of public international law. The decisions are not within the jurisdiction of the Court which may be made by a prorogation clause (see § 2.1).

12. P Pescatore, *L'ordre juridique des Communautés Européennes*, p. 174.

13. *Algera Case*, R.III:115.

14. *SNUPAT Case*, R.VII:160.

15. *ASSIDER Case*, R.I:148.

16. See *Nold Case*, R.V:110 f and *Comptoirs de Vente du Charbon de la Ruhr Case*, R.VI:910:
"... il n'appartient pas à la Cour, ... d'appliquer, *du moins directement*, les règles de droit interne, meme constitutionelles"

but,
"il y a lieu d'appliquer une règle de droit généralement admise, dans tous les pays de la Communauté",

ALMA Case, R.III:190.

17. See *The Seventh General Report of the EC*, p. 458 f.

18. *Observe that there are several different types of international organisations, and it is often difficult to ascertain their legal character.*

19. See C W Jenks, *The proper law of international organisations*.

20. This article provides that
"the decision of the Court has no binding force except between the parties and in respect of that particular case".

Part two
The Non-Contractual Liability of the Communities

Chapter four

General points concerning community liability

§ 4.1 Introduction

Article 40 (1) and (2) of the ECSC Treaty[1] provides as follows:

"Sous réserve des dispositions de l'article 34, alinéa 1, la Cour est compétente pour accorder, sur demande de la partie lésée, une réparation pécuniaire à la charge de la Communauté, en cas de préjudice causé dans l'execution du présent traité par *une faute de service* de la Communauté.

Elle est également compétente pour accorder une réparation à la charge de la Communauté en cas de préjudice causé par *une faute personnelle* d'un agent de celle-ci dans l'exercice de ses fonctions. La responsabilité personnelle des agents envers la Communauté est réglée dans les dispositions fixant leur statut ou régime qui leur est applicable".

However, the second paragraph obtained its present wording from the Merger-Treaty, article 26. It previously stated:

"Elle (la Cour) est également compéten e pour accorder une réparation à la charge d'un agent des services de la Communauté, en cas de préjudice causé par une faute personnelle de cet agent dans l'exercice de ses fonctions. Si la partie lésée n'a pu obtenir cette réparation de la part de l'agent, la Cour peut mettre une indemnité équitable à la charge de la Communauté".

The authors of the Treaties of Rome did not adopt the wording of the ECSC Treaty but modified the provisions for non-contractual liability, articles 215 (2) and 188 (2) of the EEC and the EAEC Treaties respectively. They provide as follows:

"En matière de responsabilité non contractuelle, la Communauté doit réparer, conformément aux principes généraux communs aux droits des États membres, les dommages causés par ses institutions ou par ses agents dans l'exercice de leurs fonctions. La responsabilité personnelles des agents envers la Communauté est réglée dans les dispositions fixant leur statut ou le régime qui leur est applicable".

Article 40 of the ECSC Treaty is based on the notions of *faute de service* and *faute de personnelle* which are terms directly borrowed from the French legal system, and therefore, it is here appropriate to give an outline of the French system[2].

Cases of non-contractual liability of the French state involving a *faute de serice* are entrusted to the administrative courts with the *Conseil d'État* as the final court of appeal, whereas the personal liability of civil servants for a *faute personelle* takes place before the civil courts implying acts committed in the performance of their duties as civil servants as well as private persons; liability is based on article 1382 of the *Code Civil.* In the case where the *faute personnelle* has been committed in the performance of the duties of an administration, it is possible for the personal liability and the liability of the administration to coexist.

The French administrative law requires normally the presence of *une faute* to incur liability of the state. The position of the problem is according to Waline (*opus cit.* p. 557): "Lorsque le demandeur a établi avoir souffert un préjudice et l'imputabilité de ce préjudice à une certain action (ou abstention) d'une collectivité public, ou d'un agent de celle-ci, il faut encore, pour qu'il obtienne réparation, qu'il établisse que cette action ou abstention avait le caractère d'une faute". The act causing the damage may consist of an illegal act issued by an administration as well as the omission to take action, or any other kind of measure. Concerning concrete acts one should note, on the one hand, that a legal decision can never constitute a fault, and, on the other hand, that an illegal decision not necessarily is connected with a fault, although the decision can be annulled. This may be the case concerning illegalities relating to formal requirements when the act to its content is basically justified. In principle all illegalities may give cause to a fault. Whether a fault exists or not is an appreciation *in conctreto,* taking account of all the circumstances of the case; thus according to Waline, *opus cited,* page 565: "Le Conseil d'État ne juge pas la faute d'après un critère préetabli, tel que la conduite d'un bon père de famille". The judge takes account of the seriousness of the consequences of the fault in relation to the prudence employed by the administration. When it concerns a dangerous activity in which an accident occurs the administration is expected to have acted more cautiously than normally. When the fault of the administration has been established one can also say (Rivero, *opus cit.* p. 249) there is a *faute de service* on the part of the administration which expresses the existence of "une défaillance dans le fonctionnement normal de service".

The distinctive feature of the *faute de service* is that it is not attributable to individual civil servants of the administration but to the administration itself. Furthermore, although the French system of state liability does not apply the standard of the *bonus pater familias* the notion of *faute de service* nevertheless contains elements contiguous to the notion of *culpa (Verschulden).* Rivero, *opus cited,* page 249, states the following concerning the normal functioning of a service: "De tout service, on est fondé à attendre un certain niveau moyen, variable d'ailleurs selon sa mission et selon les circonstances; la faute apparait au-dessous de ce niveau".

Not every *faute de service* entails the obligation to repair a damage, since in some instances the fault must have a certain gravity which depends on the service concerned; there are three degrees: simple or ordinary fault, serious fault and exceptional gravity of fault. Furthermore, the circumstances may change the appreciation of the fault in the sense that an act which during normal times would be classified as *faute lourde,* in war times would only be considered as *faute simple.* The existence and the degrees of a fault is very much a matter of appreciation of the actual case. Furthermore, it is up to the victim to prove the existence of the fault and the damage resulting from it, but in certain cases it is presumed a fault by the administration from which it may exonerate by proof of *force majeure,* a fault committed by the victim or actions taken by third parties.

It seems, however, irrational if the authors of the Treaties of Rome had wanted to adopt the system of the ECSC Treaty, to use a different wording to that in these Treaties; therefore it is proper to suppose that the authors of these Treaties had the intention in some way of changing the extension of and/or the conditions for rendering the liability of these Communities in relation to the older adopted system of the ECSC Treaty, which also seems perfectly feasible with regard to the different natures of the Treaties. Concerning the new wording of article 40 (2) of the ECSC Treaty it is probably the expression of the wish to achieve the same conditions for the civil servants of all three Communities which should be seen in the light of the merger of the Executives. The Community now assumes the liability for the civil servants in relation to third parties. The modification must be considered as a step removed from the French legal system.

Article 34 of the ECSC Treaty is a *lex specialis* of the community liability in relation to article 40; if the Court has annulled an act and if the plaintiff has suffered a direct and special damage from the decision or recommendation concerned and the Court finds the act involving a fault of such a nature as to engage the responsibility of the Community, the High Authority shall assure an equitable repair of the suffered damage and if necessary pay a fair indemnity. The Advocate-General Lagrange stated in the *Meroni Case* (R. VII:351) that when an annulled decision has caused damage and when the measures of implementation of the judgement are not sufficient, the article shall assure a satisfactory compensation. An action for indemnity on the basis of this article is only open to enterprises or groups of enterprises in the sense of article 80 (see artt. 33 (2) and 35 (1)). If the High Authority omits to take the required measures to comply with the decision of annulment, an action for indemnity may be brought before the Court (art. 34 (2)). All illegal measures even if they are annulled by the Court do not render *ipso facto* a right for indemnity, as the indemnity is not a punishment but the repair of a damage resulting from a basically unjustified measure (Advocate-General Roemer in the *Kergall Case,* R. II:48). Moreover, the omission to act of the High Authority, i.e. the implied decision not to act (art. 35), may be challenge in an action for annulment. The relationship between articles 34 and 40 shall be dealt with in § 6.1.

The questions relating to illegal acts have not been treated in the same way in the Treaties of Rome as to that of the ECSC Treaty. According to article 176 (1) of the EEC Treaty the institution whose act has been declared void (or failure to act being contrary to the Treaty) by the Court shall take measures to comply with the judgement, but this obligation does not affect (art. 176 (2)) obligations following from article 215 (2).

Because of the different wording in the provisions for non-contractual liability in the ECSC Treaty and the EEC and the EAEC Treaties it was at least theoretically an open question, before the Court had expressed its view on the matter, whether the provisions incorporated in the Treaties of Rome also included a committed fault or not, rendering the liability of the Communities. A fault was pointed out to be a necessary requisite in the *Kampffmeyer Case* (R.XIII:339). The case-law relating to the liability of the ECSC was made earlier than those of the EEC and EAEC, and the former has certainly excercised influence on the latter. However, one should note that the relevant provisions of the Rome Treaties do not contain a reference to *faute de service* or any such references but afford to the Court a broader basis in developing the liability system of those Communities.

The starting point in determining the extent of and the conditions for the non-contractual liability of all three Communities are the notions of *faute de service* and *faute de personnelle* as revealed by the case-laws pertaining to the Treaties but some preliminary matters should first be settled.

§ 4.2 The jurisdiction of the Court

During the old wording of article 40 (2) of the ECSC Treaty, the Court was competent when a civil servant of the Community was sued for indemnity on the ground of a fault commited in carrying out his duties; in fact, a servant has however never been sued. According to the new wording of article 40 (2) the Community may be sued before the Court for indemnity because of faults committed by its servants in carrying out their duties; in this respect, the competence of the Court nowadays is identical with the one stipulated in the Treaties of Rome. A civil servant[3] committing a fault in carrying out his duties, or according to the Rome Treaties causing damage in performing his duties is only responsible towards the Community according to the staff regulation; no action brought by the injured party will lie against him personally in the Court or in national courts. Moreover, the servants enjoy immunity under the *Protocol on Privileges and Immunities of the European*

Communities, according to article 12, for their official capacity. However, an institution may waive the immunity accorded to an official when it is not contrary to the interest of the Communities.

If damage is caused by a civil servant when not carrying out his duties nothing will save him from being sued before a national court (artt. 40 (3) ECSC, 183 EEC and 155 EAEC). It may nevertheless be difficult for the national court to decide, whether the servant has acted in carrying out his duties or not, but this problem is solved by a reference to the Court which is obliged to give a preliminary ruling on the matter[4].

The Court is further exclusively competent to judge on a *faute de service* imputable to the ECSC or *damage caused by its institutions* of the EEC and EAEC in carrying out the Treaties. It seems the Communities may be sued before national courts for indemnity, when article 40 (1) and (2) ECSC, articles 178 and 215 (2) EEC and 151 and 188 (2) EAEC Treaties are not applicable, which follows from articles 40 (3) ECSC, 183 EEC and 155 EAEC Treaties, although it is difficult to imagine what kind of situations there might be[5]. If a national court is uncertain as to its competence in this respect it may refer the case for a preliminary ruling to the Court. In a few cases national courts have touched upon the non-contractual liability of the Communities inasmuch as declaring themselves incompetent[6].

However, the possibility of conflict of jurisdiction may remain, but if the community law and jurisdiction are given priority over national laws equality of law is saved. In this context, it should be observed that a judgement of a national court must be submitted to the Court which has exclusive authority to allow execution against the Communities[7]. Finally, it should be mentioned that the provisions giving competence to national courts certainly mean the national courts of the Member-States. Note, the English version of the Rome Treaties expressly states the national courts of the Member-States. Moreover, the Communities will probably enjoy immunity of jurisdiction in most other states in force of their character of international public organisations.

§ 4.3 Persons entitled to bring an action for indemnity before the court

In the *Vloeberghs Case* (R. VII:426) the Court stated that moral or physical persons not being subjects to the ECSC Treaty could also claim indemnity for suffered damage caused by a *faute de service* committed in the carrying out the Treaty. Accordingly the limitations provided for in articles 33 and 35 do not apply to article 40.

Concerning the Treaties of Rome the provisions in question only say that the Communities shall make good damage caused by their institutions and their civil servants in carrying out their duties; from article 173 one cannot draw the conclusion that a group or groups of persons should be excluded in general from lodging actions for indemnity.

From the case-law one is, however, inclined to conceive that all persons including foreign enterprises (see the *ICI Case*, R.XVIII:620 which concerned annulment of a decision taken by the Commission pursuant to art. 85) and citizens (see the case of *Alvis*, R.IX:97) in the Member-States as well as such persons domiciled in third countries are allowed to bring indemnity actions invoking they have suffered damage in such a manner provided for in the Rome Treaties. This could probably be extended to apply also to the ECSC Treaty.

§ 4.4 Institutions, civil servants and other agents of the Communities

4.4.1 The ECSC Treaty

Here the question is raised concerning which institutions, civil servants and other agents of the Community may engage its liability. The Community is a moral person according to article 6 of the Treaty and is represented by its institutions; from that it follows that any case of *faute de service* of an institution must be imputed to the Community. The institutions are according to article 7 the High Authority (Commission) which has been a party before the Court in many cases, the Assembly which was a party in the *Algera Case* (R. III:129), the Council and the Court[8]. The judges and the Advocates-General seem in principle at least to be able to render the Community liable by a *faute personnelle* (see the *Colotti Case*, R.X:886).

A member of the Commission can be forced to retire by the Court (see articles 10 and 13 of the Merger-Treaty) if he breaches the obligations imposed on him in his office or if he is guilty of a serious misconduct, and it is possible that these, his breach and misconduct, may imply the committing of a *faute personnelle* of which the Community could be liable.

Concerning politicians both within the Council and the Parliament the situation is to an extent more precarious; according to article 9 of the Protocol on the Privileges and Immunities of the European Communities the members of the Parliament shall not be subject to any form of legal proceedings in respect of views expressed or votes cast by them in the performance of their duties. If such a member of the Parliament performs actions similar to those of a normal civil servant, it seems possible that he is able to commit a *faute personnelle* which may render the Community liable. The members of the Council are not civil servants of the Communities and will not render the liability unless they could be construed as agents of the Communities.

Moreover, all civil servants of the Communities may incur the Communities' liability through a committed *faute personnelle*. The Court declared in the *Chasse Case* (R.VIII:737): "...le fonctionnaire de ministère néerlandais des affaires économiques ... n'est pas un subordonné de la Haute Autorité et n'en a pas reçu d'ordres, mais qu'il a agi en sa qualité de fonctionnaire national", though he was involved in the equalisation system of scrap iron together with the High Autority. In the same system auxilary organs to the High Authority as *L'Office des consommateurs des ferrailles* have been considered by the Court as a kind of agent of the High Authority for which the latter and consequently the Community was responsible. The Court wrote in the *Meroni Case* (R.VII:339) that "... car elles pourraient révéler l'existence d'une faute de service de la Haute Autorité ou, ce qui reviendrait au meme, des organismes de Bruxelles". In the *Worms Case* (R.VIII:398) the Court drew up firmer limits of responsibility concerning the auxilary organs: "... dans l'exercice de son activité proprement commerciale, l'O.C.C.F., société belge de droit privé, est régie par le droit interne; que ce n'est que dans les cas où les agissements de l'O.C.C.F. concernent le fonctionnement du mécanisme de péréquation, et ont de ce chef un caractère de service public, qu'ils peuvent etre considérés comme engageant directement la responsabilité de la Haute Autorité".

4.4.2 The EEC and EAEC Treaties

The Communities shall make good damage caused by their institutions or by their civil servants in carrying out their duties; the institutions are, probably also the Economic and Social Committee in this context which is supported by the wording of the *Convention relating to certain institutions common to the European Communities,* articles 1, 3 and 5, the Council, the Commission, the Parliament and the Court; for example the Parliament was a party in the case of *Lasalle* (R.X:63), the Commission of *Plaumann Case* (R.IX:199), the Court in the case of *Colotti* (R.X:886) and the Council in the case of *Gorter* (R.VII:540). The European Investment Bank seems in this context to be excluded even if the notion of "institutions" is very broadly interpreted. In the *Werhahn Case* the plaintiffs had claimed (R.1973:1233) that the Council and the Commission were jointly responsible while the defendants thought that because of that the actions were inadmissible. The Court took the view (page 1246) that since the Community was represented by its institutions, it should accordingly be represented before the Court by the institution responsible for the contested measures regardless of article 211, which deals with the legal capacity and the representation of the Community in the legal systems of the Member-States. The plaintiffs' claims, however, did not make the actions inadmissible, and in this case it was correct to sue the Community represented by both the Council and the Commission.

However, one should note the recently formed international entity called the European Monetary Cooperation Fund where a reference concerning non-contractual liability (art. 9 of the Annex) is made to article 215 of the EEC Treaty. One may from that assume that the Court is the competent *fora* although there is no express reference. In this context one also notes the Supply Agency of Euratom which also has its own legal personality. Both the Fund and the Agency are thus distinct entities from the Communities' and cannot be considered as institutions as such. The question which arises is whether they might be considered as agents of an institution which therefore assumes its liability or whether they will assume their own liability. The relevant criterion when the institution assumes liability seems then to be, regarding the case-law of the ECSC Treaty, that the body concerned is subordinate to the will of an institution from which it takes orders and as the enlarged arm of the institution is performing a public function. Here there appears a difference between these bodies; the Fund is governed by a Board of Governors and shall act in accordance with the directives adopted by the Council (article 2 of the Statute), while the Agency pursuant to article 53 (1) of the EAEC Treaty is supervised by the Commission which can address directives to it and possesses a right of veto to its decisions. Furthermore there are no provisions for a liability specifically pertaining to the Agency neither in the Treaty nor in its Statute. It seems then that the Agency is a subordinate agent of the Commission and will through that fact engage the liability of the Community. In a dispute which was settled outside any court or other formal proceedings the Agency had to pay contractual indemnity which was paid out of community funds. This is understandable since the Agency is devoid of the necessary economic resources with a capital amounting merely to 3.200.000 units of account. The Fund on the other hand seems to assume its own liabilities but can of course be held jointly responsible with the Council (the Community).

Footnotes chapter four

1. Note that the French language is the only official one, the relevant articles of the Treaties of Rome are also kept in that language.

2. See J Rivero, *Droit administratif,* p. 239 f and M Waline, *Précis de droit administratif,* p. 558 f. All the national systems concerning state liability are of course of interest, and references will be made to them where appropriate.
See also the interesting views concerning the *faute de service* by W Much, *Die Amtshaftung im Recht der Europäischen Gemeinschaft für Kohle und Stahl,* p. 26 f.

3. See, Statut des fonctionnaires des Communautés européennes et régime appli-, cable aux autres agents des Communautés article 91 (8) 1 which makes the court competent to judge any dispute between the Communities and their civil servants (cf. art. 179 of the EEC Treaty, art. 152 of the EAEC Treaty and art. 42 of the ECSC Treaty).

4. Although the system appears in principle to be easy to operate there are certain complications such as the immunity from jurisdiction of the civil servants. In the *Sayag Case* (R.XIV:575) the Court pronounced concerning a question forwarded by the *Cour de Cassation de Belgique* that the immunity of jurisdiction applied to actions "qui, par leur nature, représentent une participation de celui qui invoque l'immunité à l'exercice des taches de l'institution dont il relève". The Court also said that the qualification of an action to enjoy immunity or not did not prejudge the matter of responsibility of the Community. The same court later asked the Court in the same case (*Sayag Case*, R.XV:329) concerning the meaning of a civil servant's performance of his duties which the Court considered to be an action of a direct and internal relationship with the necessary extension of the tasks entrusted to the institution.

5. The Court referred to this possibility and art. 40 (3) in the *Vloeberghs Case* (R.VII:427).

6. See, Antwerp Meat Import *versus* État Belge (Conseil d'État 19.9.1972, Recueil, 1972, pp. 686—690) and Comptoir agricole des pays-bas normands *versus* ONIC (Conseil d'État de la France, 4.2.1969, Recueil 1969, pp. 610—611).

7. Art. 1 of the Protocol on Privileges and Immunities of the European Communities.

8. The Court cannot be sued before itself by a plaintiff invoking the damaging effects from an earlier judgement of the Court. Cf. the modification of a judgement by exceptional forms of recourse. In the national legal systems the courts normally assume no liability for their mistakes but the judges themselves may on certain conditions.

Chapter five

The notion of faute de service

§ 5.1 The ECSC Treaty

The Court has not had much to refer to in the Treaty in elaborating the notion of *faute de service* other than article 47 (4) providing that "la violation par la Haute Autorité du secret professionnel ayant causé un dommage à une entreprise" is a basis for an action according to article 40. Furthermore, it follows from article 34 that the annulment of an illegal act as such does not automatically constitute a fault of such a nature as to incur the responsibility of the Community.

Faute de service is a term which cannot be explained by a few words as a wrongful act committed on behalf of the Community, but one should proceed to a closer examination as to its constitution. The case-law by the Court is so far concerned with cases relating to actions for indemnity brought by the civil servants of the Community and actions for indemnity lodged by coal and steel undertakings mainly pertaining to the equalisation system for imported scrap iron. The system was instituted by the High Authority in 1954 and was based on article 53 b of the Treaty. The purpose of the system was to assure the regular provisioning of iron to the Common Market, since the resources within the market were insufficient. All the consuming enterprises of the market had to pay contributions calculated on the basis of their consumption of iron; the contributions were, in principle, designed to permit the payment of equalisation subsidies to enterprises which had acquired expensive imported iron from third countries. The High Authority was in charge of the system but had conferred responsibility upon *L'Office commun des consommateurs des ferailles* (called *L'Office*) and *La Caisse de péréquation des ferrailles importées* (called *La Caisse*) which formed the so-called *organismes de Bruxelles* and were *sociétés cooperatives* under Belgian law; in each Member-State there were also regional offices.

As a consequence of the judgement in the case of *Meroni versus the High Authority* (R.IV:16) the delegation of powers of decision to *L'Office* and *La Caisse* was withdrawn by the High Authority from August 1, 1958 and the Authority assumed direct responsibility for the system. The compulsory equalisation system ended November 30, 1958, until which date more than 13 million tons of iron had been imported and subjected to the equalisation system. In the summer of 1956 there were rumours circulating concerning the possible existence of frauds and irregularities in the system. Defects were also discovered, and several actions have been brought before the Court on this subject. However, the High Authority tried to rectify the weaknesses of the system and in its 9th general report in 1961 the High Authority presented the actions taken with a view to controlling the origin of the iron admissible to equalisation. It appears *inter alia* from the report that 229.889 tons of the total amount of 13.018.270 tons had been unduly admitted to equalisation, that the irregularities consisted of many different types and had been committed in several Member-States and that it was impossible to estimate the sums paid unduly. In the 10th, 11th and 12th general reports of the High Authority indications have been given to actions taken concerning the liquidation of the system and the control of the iron subjected to equalisation. The general decision 19/65 by the High Authority laid down the rules for establishing definite calculations for iron submitted to equalisation and definite fixation of the sums of contributions and rates of interests. However, the system is not yet completed, see the *ECSC Auditors Report* for the year 1973 (Paul Gaudy).

Until now one can distinguish the following categories of *faute de service* which emerge from in particular the following cases:

1) Bad organisation of the services

The Feram Case (R. V:506) in which the Court examined whether the High Authority had committed a *faute de service* according to article 40 ". . . du fait de ne pas avoir mieux organisé le système d'établissement des certificats d'orgine, pour la ferraille bénéficiant de versements de péréquation". The abuse occurred indicated a defective and insufficient organisation. The deliverance of certificates had been entrusted to a national ministry which seemed to offer the best guarantees against all misuse and considering the circumstances one could not blame the High Authority for adopting the system.

The Meroni Case (R.VII:325) in which the Court examined whether successive rectifications of the sums to be paid as contributions to the equalisation system were due to *une organisation défectueuse des services ou des travaux administratifs* but did not find that to be the case.

2) Defective management or function of the services

The Feram Case (R.V:506); the absence of adequate control did not constitute a fault in this case, see above.

The Meroni Case (R.VII:325) in which the Court examined whether certain delays of notifications of equalisation contributions and rectifications thereof revealed *une gestion négligente*. The Court did not think so, since the plaintiffs had not shown the existence of inexcusable errors.

The Five Lille Case (R.VII:559) in which the Court made the High Authority responsible for false promises given by *L'Office* as to payments of subsidies for costs of transportation which were contrary to the Treaty. The promises were due to the fact that the High Authority had "...gravement négligé les devoirs de surveillance qu'une diligence normale lui imposait, faute qui engendre sa responsabilité".

The Laminoirs Case (R.XI:1124) concerned the same promises as in the Five Lille Case, and the Court stated that "le manque de diligence de la Haute Autorité est devenu progressivement manifeste". The Court charged the High Authority with *fautes de service* incurring its liability. In this case the plaintiffs considered the damage as an effect of the lack of supervision instead of claiming indemnity equivalent to the subsidies which had been refused to them by the High Authority.

In the *Laminoirs Case* (R.XII:200) the Court accorded indemnity to five enterprises and the actions of the remaining nine were dismissed, since those companies were not considered to have suffered any damage.

The Temple Case (R.IX:589) from which it implicitly follows that a certain conduct or behaviour of the High Authority that led the plaintiff into an erroneous conviction being to his detriment may constitute a *faute de service*. The Court proceeded to examine the *causal link* between the fault and the alleged damage. To that end the Court stated that one should not only take account of whether the conduct in fact had induced an error in the mind of the plaintiff but also if it could and should have caused such an error in the mind of a prudent person. The Court did not find such a direct causual link to exist.

The Espérance-Longdoz Case (R.XI:1322) in which the plaintiff alleged the High Authority to have committed a *faute de service* in neglecting or omitting to inform the plaintiff of the nature of certain iron, which was to the plaintiff's detriment, though having the knowledge of the problems involved. As the prudent person the plaintiff was he could not have ignored the prevailing situation, and considering the circumstances one could not blame the High Authority for not having taken any action.

The Forges de Chantillon Case (R.XII:266) in which a decision by the High Authority was contrary to prior information conveyed. The deliverance of the wrong information was alleged to constitute a *faute de service*. Since the plaintiff was not considered to have suffered any damage from the contested behaviour, there was no need for examining the existence of a *faute de service*.

The Simet and Feram Cases (R.XVII:197 and 227) in which the plaintiffs claimed the late notifications of their contributions to the equalisation system to be to their detriment and to constitute a *faute de service*. The calculation *à posteriori* was inherent in the system and could not give cause to indemnity. As a second fault the High Authority was said to have seriously violated its duty of supervision which had facilitated the occurence of enormous frauds. The existence of frauds did not prove by themselves a failure of the administration in this respect.

The Algera Case (R.III:86) in which the Court established that "Cette remise (of a decision) prématurée et intempestive constitue une faute de service, par le fait qu'elle a créé une situation fausse sous des apparences légales". Another *faute de service* had been committed through "les tergiversations de la partie défenderesse envers les demandeurs".

Leroy Case (R.IX:399) in which the Court stated that *critiques superfétatoires* with respect to a civil servant contained in a legally valid decision may constitute a fault.

3) Illegalities through

A) Positive acts

The Algera Case (R.III:86) in which the Court established that "le retrait de l'admission au Statut ayant été illégal" formed a *faute de service* which entailed a right to reparation according to article 40 of the Treaty.

The Kergall Case (R.II:15) in which the Court did not annul the decision not to renew the plaintiff's employment contract but established that the decision of non-renewal involved irregularities which the defendant had committed in exercising its function, and therefore constituted a fault incurring its liability.

B) Omission

The Vloebergs Case (R.VII:395) in which the Court stated that "il est certain que la violation du traité reprochée à la Haute Autorité comme inhérente à son inaction peut etre invoquée à l'appui d'une action fondée sur l'article 40". Furthermore, the Court firstly examined whether the lack of action of the High Authority, although the omission as such might constitute a *faute de service,* had violated the plaintiff's interests in such a way as to entitle him to reparation of allegedly suffered damage. The rules obliging the High Authority to act had only been created to the protection of the interests of the undertakings being subjects to the Treaty and the Member-States, and since the plaintiff was not such an undertaking, he could not invoke in this case the inaction of the High Authority.

In summarising the case-law as to the *faute de service* one should first incidently note that in all Member-States but the exception of France the *culpa-rule (Verschulden)* is generally applied[1] although there are exceptions where e.g. the *culpa* is presumed to charge the administration; these systems for state liability are built on analogies from the civil ones of tortious liability. The French system which has previously been described was detached from the civil one provided for by the *Code Civil* through the famous case of *Blanco* by the *Tribunal des Conflits* (Recueil 1873 S 61) which case still remains the basis of the autonomy of the French system of state liability. One should however note that the French system retains elements of the *culpa* in the notion of *faute de service* although of a particular nature which do not fully correspond to civil concepts.

In the early case of *Algera* (R.III:128) the Court stated that it was not necessary to examine "si la faute de service, au sens de l'article 40 du Traité, présuppose le dol ou tout au moins une négligence coupable, ou si toute attitude illégale—meme inconsciente—de la part d'une institution peut tomber sous le coup de ladite notion". The Advocate-General Lagrange objected in his submissions in the *Feram Case* (R.V:527) to this way of reasoning as to an objective liability. In the case of *Meroni* (R.VII:339) the situation concerning the fault was further enlightened through the Court's statement:"... il convient cependant d'examiner si ces erreurs étaient susceptibles d'etre évitées par une bonne administration, car elles pourraient révéler l'existence d'une faute de service de la Haute Autorité". In addition the Advocate-General Lagrange established in the *Chasse Case* (R.VIII:751) that the basis of article 40 was the *faute de service* which, was a *résponsabilité subjectif et la faute doit etre établi.*

The conclusion as to the constitution of the *faute de service* that emerges would thus be, that any objective fact, e.g. those exposed by the case-law, which can be attributed to the administration, may be invoked by the plaintiff to make a *faute de service* from which he has suffered damage. The crucial point is that the alleged mistake must be declared to constitute a *faute de service*[2], and this will only happen when the alleged mistake could have been avoided by a good administration regarding the actual circumstances of the particular case. The failure of the administration in not meeting the requirements of a good administration in a certain position and at a certain time, thus also including the nature of the service and the means of implementation entrusted, constitutes the fault and makes the responsibility to a subjective one. Here one can also perceive the concepts of the *Verschulden* and of the cupability[3].

As has been mentioned above, the French system contains faults of different degrees, and certain activities or duties have been labelled as to the degree required of the fault to incur liability, for example police-brutalities require a serious fault as well as in general activities performed by tax-authorities and hospitals. The question which should be answered is whether the Court has observed the different degrees of a fault, or not. One notes that the wording in article 34 (1) "... une faute de nature à engager la responsabilité de la Communauté" refers to the degrees of the fault. Since most cases concern the equalisation system the question is pertinent whether the Court has regarded this specific activity to be a very difficult one requiring a particular or serious fault instead of a simple fault. In the two cases where the Court has established the existence of *faute de service* it employed different wordings; in the *Five Lille Case* (R.VII:592) the High Authority was found to have "gravement négligé les devoirs de surveillance" which was incumbent upon it by normal diligence. And in the *Laminoirs Case* (R.XI:1157) the Court wrote "le manque de diligence de la Haute Autorité est devenu progressivement manifeste" and the illegal promises were attributable to *fautes de service* "de nature à engager sa responsabilité".

In those two cases the basic facts were the same and it seems doubtfully to attribute any significance to the word *gravement* mentioned in the *Five Lille Case*. If thus the Court has been silent, on the one hand, the Advocates-General, on the other hand, have more frequently in their submissions expressed opinions concerning the existence of the various degrees of the fault required. In the *Meroni Case* (R.VII:348) the Advocate-General Lagrange pronounced that concerning the equalisation system it sufficed with an ordinary fault to render the Community responsible. In the *Chasse Case* (R.VIII:753) he distinguished between *un service de gestion* and *un service de controle* of which the former required a simple fault since the administration in that case is more directly involved whilst the latter required *une faute lourde*. The Advocate-General Roemer thought in the *Vloeberghs Case* (R.VII:469) that "D'après le droit administratif francais, en cas de carence, lorsque l'administration n'a pas exercé son role de surveillance, la 'faute lourde' est une condition pour engager la responsabilité" which was applicable in that case. In the case of *Espérance-Longdoz* (R.XI:1360) he did not find the existence of a *faute grave*. Furthermore, one should note that the Court has never established a fault and considered it—due to its degree—to be insufficient to incur liability. If the Court has established a fault, it has so far always entailed liability otherwise no fault has been found to exist. One could accordingly doubt whether the Court has deliberately counted with the degrees of a fault in relation to preclassified activities for incurring liability on the part of the Community. The working formula by the Court seems then to be that if the Court considers there are sufficient reasons pursuant to its discretionary appreciation of the facts involved, to charge the administration with a fault, the Court plainly states the existence of a fault incurring liability. The decisive element in the discretionary considerations seems to be the fair balancing of the interests of the individuals and the necessity of performing the activities of the Community provided for in the Treaty, see the statement of Advocate-General Lagrange in the *Meroni Case* (R.VII:347) and the Court's general reasoning in the *Simet Case* (R.XVII:213f).

Some of the special problems involved with regard to illegal concrete acts shall here be indicated. An act may be illegal due to the different defects tainted to it and the basis for challenging an act is article 33 of the Treaty which is supplemented by article 35. The illegality is normally the first condition for entailing liability but all illegal acts do not; this is achieved by different means in the various Member-States. The Advocate-General

Roemer expressed in the *Kergall Case* (R.II:48) that ". . . une violation de la forme n'a d'importance que si elle a exercé une influence sur le contenu de la décision elle-meme"[4]. It directly follows from article 34 (1) that although an act has been annulled by the Court, it must be declared to involve a fault of such a serious nature as to incur liability. The establishment of the objective mistake i.e. the annulment of the act concerned is not sufficient but the fault has to be recognised, it is to say the act is due to a seriously bad administration[5]. Unfortunately, there are so far no cases relating to the application of article 34 in this respect. The gravity of the fault required for incurring liability is not indicated but has been left to the Court to decide. In an analysis made by Walter Much[6], he suggested some hypotheses in that respect such as the misuse of power automatically incurring liability and similarly in cases where the High Authority uses its power inadequately so that the decision falls outside of what may be expected by a normally good administration, and finally, where there is negligence on the part of the administration, considering the diligence and prudence which one might normally expect from an administration in charge of important interests.

§ 5.2 The EEC and EAEC Treaties

Opinions differed regarding the importance of the ECSC system to the interpretation and development of the system under the Treaties of Rome, thus Advocate-General Lagrange pronounced in *Common Market Law Review 1965/66,* page 32, that the EEC Treaty was "making a choice and taking over the essence of the system enshrined in article 40 of the ECSC Treaty—in other words the French system". Léon Goffin wrote in *Droit des Communautés Eruopéennes 1969,* page 156, "cela parait d'autant moins certain que ce dernier article 40 exige expressément une faute". Furthermore, the Advocate-General Roemer declared in the case of *Plaumann* (R.IX:242) that the Court had avoided narrowly basing itself on the French law but developed the law of the Community as "une directrice semblable à celle de l'article 215 (2), alinéa 2".

However, the development of the case-law will appear from the summary below, and the Court has considered the following circumstances to be susceptible to incur liability:

1) Defective management or function of the services
The van Stenwijk Case (R.X:639) in which the cancellation of the plaintiff's employment contract was not considered by the Court to be illegal. It could only give cause to indemnity if it contained superflous criticisms of the person concerned which in this case the decision did not.

The Richez-Parise Case (R.XVI:325) in which the Commission had given the plaintiff wrong information. The Court stated that the inexact interpretation of a community rule of law did not normally itself constitute a *faute de service*. However, a rectification by the Commission had been possible in April 1968 but had been delayed towards the end of the same year without reason. This omission incurred the community liability.

The Fiehn Case (R.XVI:547) in which the circumstances were the same as in the above case.

The Labeyrie Case (R.XIV:431) which concerned the possible existence of damage caused to the plaintiff's reputation. The Court did not think so, and stated that the service concerned had acted with "la circonspection nécessaire et exclusive de faute".

The Compagnie Continentale Case (R.1975:117) in which the Council had adopted a resolution in order to inform the concerned merchants of a new system of subsidies to be instituted in the agricultural field. The plaintiff thought the information delivered to be misleading which had led him to commit errors to his own detriment. The Court took the view that the Council through omitting to insert into the resolution certain reservations had falsified the mission of information which incurred the community liability. The Court proceeded to examine the causal link between the Council's behaviour and the alleged prejudice and employed the same test as in the *Temple Case* (see above § 5.1) with the same result.

2) Illegalities through

A) Positive acts

The Luhleich Case (R.XI:728) in which the Court established that the decision to cancel the plaintiff's employment contract was attached to procedural vices and the unfavourable information thereby obtained against the plaintiff was inexact and incompletely alleged. The decision was therefore illegal and, furthermore, it constituted a fault of such a nature as to incur liability. Since the plaintiff did not wish to return to the service of the Commission, the Court thought there was no reason to annul the decision but only to accord indemnity.

The Willame Case (R.XI:804) in which the procedure foregoing the cancellation of the plaintiff's employment contract was attached to substantial vices and therefore was annulled. This was due to the abuse of power and the ignorance of elementary provisions in the staff regulation by a high functionary. The irregularities committed by the Commission constituted a fault which had also caused moral damage to the plaintiff for which he was granted indemnity.

*The Kampffmeyer Case** (R.XIII:318) concerned an annulled decision taken by the Commission.

The Becker Case (R.XIII:370) similar to the Kampffmeyer Case.

*The Schöppenstedt Case** (R.XVII:975) concerned a non-annulled normative act.

*The Compagnie d'approvisionnement (CIE)** (R.XVIII:391) concerned non-annulled normative acts.

*The Haegeman Case** (R.XVIII:1005) concerned non-annulled acts.

*The Wünsche Case** (R.1973:791) concerned a non-annulled normative act.

*The Merkur Case** (R.1973:1055) concerned a non-annulled normative acts.

*The Werhahn Case** (R.1973:1229) concerned non-annulled normative acts.

*The Holtz & Willemsen Case** (R.1974:675) concerned non-annulled normative acts.

*The Comptoir national technique agricole (CNTA) Case** (R.1975:533) concerned a non-annulled normative act.

B) Omission

*The Lütticke Case** (R.XVII:325) concerned the infringement of the Treaty by omission committed by the Commission.

It appears from the case-law that various actions committed by the administrations of the community institutions together with a fault also within the framework of the Treaties of Rome have been able to constitute a *faute de service* incurring community liability[7]. However, there are some very intricate questions pertinent to the fault and the *faute de service* concept in the context of illegal acts which come forth in particular from the recent cases of the Court, and one should therefore proceed to a closer examination of the relevant cases in this respect.

The cases of *Luhleich and Willame* seem both to be quite clear in this respect, i.e. the illegal decisions were recognised as faults incurring community liability.

In the cases of *Kampffmeyer* (R.XIII:318) and *Becker* (R.XIII:370) the Court considered a decision of the Commission which previously had been declared illegal, due to abuse of power, and annulled in the *Toepfer Case* (R.XI:525). This decision constituted an erroneous application of article 22 of regulation 19/1961; the Commision had applied article 22 under unjustified circumstances and in order to rectify a difficult situation resulting from the application of a zero-tax-level brought damage to the interests of the importers although having knowledge of the applications for licences based on information delivered pursuant to community rules. The described behaviour of the Commission constituted a *faute de service* incurring the Community's liability. The fault was mainly composed by "un comportement

· See Annex 1 for summaries of these cases.

68

d'ensemble qui s'est essentiellement manifesté par l'utilisation abusive faite de l'article 22, dont certains termes d'ailleurs décisifs ont été méconnus".

The Advocate-General Gand was of the opinion (page 355f) that the Commission had been negligent in taking the decision which endowed to it the character of a fault; the decision had been taken without sufficient considerations. Furthermore, he plainly pronounced in the *Becker Case* (R.XIII:392) that the Court in the *Kampffmeyer Case* had judged the Commission's decision to constitute a *faute de service* susceptible of incurring the community liability. The Court maintained its wording from the *Kampffmeyer Case* in the *Becker Case,* and one could then summarise, that the fault was not due to a misapprehension of the facts involved but the Commission had taken the decision carelessly without due considerations when disregarding important requirements relating to article 22 of the concerned regulation[8].

Hence these cases clearly show that the Court at that time formally and substantially counted with a fault that had to be recognised which evidently means an alignment to the ECSC system i.e. an illegality does not automatically incur liability (see art. 34). However, the *Lütticke Case* (R.XVII:325) commences a development which puts doubts into the picture concerning the importance of a fault, although these indications were interrupted by two subsequent cases. In the *Lütticke Case* consideration 10 on page 337 reveals the questions of whether the necessity of a fault has been abolished, or a fault has not to be shown but may be presumed as a matter of course when the illegality is established, or if a certain illegality in itself shall imply a fault, since the Court when pronouncing itself upon the criteria for community liability did not mentioned the fault. In this case there was no concrete decision but *un carence* to consider which may as well involve an illegality inasmuch as it is an infringement of the Treaty or any other rule of law relating to its application (cf. the *Vloeberghs Case*). The plaintiff alleged to the Court that the Commission had omitted to direct a decision or a directive to the German Republic with a view to bringing a disputed tax in conformity with the principles established in articles 95 and 97 of the EEC Treaty. The obligations of the Commission were to exercise surveillance in finding out whether or not the German legislation was in conformity with the Treaty concerning the tax level and if not, to direct a decision to the German Republic. It appeared that the Commission had notified the competent German authorities, and what is more, found the tax to be rather high and had tried to lower it, which also was achieved later on. Considering the circumstances the Commission did not find it opportune to take immediately a decision to that effect. The Court held the view that the Commission had not failed in its surveillance and furthermore the tax rate did not exceed the limits emanating from the relevant articles in the Treaty; accordingly there had been no reason for the Commission to take a decision and thus there was no omission violating the Treaty.

Concerning the omission by the Court in the *Lütticke Case* to mention the fault, L Goffin and M Mahieu thought in *Cahiers 1972*, page 86, that this was due to a matter of phrasing rather than substance, since "Ce que la Cour a entendu analyser, c'est à l'évidence le caractère 'fautif' du comportement de la Commission, tel qu'il lui était soumis". Therefore, one should not attach any particular meaning to this case. Furthermore, they considered in general an illegality by which the administration had disregarded a rule of law for its conduct, to constitute a fault.

Suppose that the Commission had interpreted the Treaty in an erroneous way in finding the German legislation to be in conformity with the Treaty and because of that had not taken a decision, while the Court had taken the opposite view. It is not improbable that liability may be excluded in such a case, since according to the laws of the Member-States, when the interpretation is due to an excusable error of law, such considerations are taken into account; this was discussed in the submissions of the Advocate-General in the case of *Kampffmeyer*. However, these considerations are inherent in the notion of the *faute de service* insofar as the fault is related to what is expected by a good administration in the concrete case. In this context one notes the statement in the case of *Richez-Paris* (R.XVI:339 and 340) that the inexact interpretation of a regulation itself did not constitute a *faute de service* but the omission to rectify it did, once the mistake was discovered.

In the case of *Schöppenstedt* the plaintiff alleged that there was a *faute de service* by the Council in violating community law and in particular in violating a rule having the character of a *Schutznorm* when establishing rules for compensating price-differences between the national markets and the community market; the infringement was due to a *culpa* by the Council which should have known before adopting the contested regulation the problems of the German sugar industries. The main question was whether the action could be accepted, since the alleged illegality concerned a non-annulled normative act involving choices as to economic policy issued by the Council. In the splendid submissions by the Advocate-General Roemer, he concluded the affirmative in considering the laws of the Member-States whereby he referred *inter alia* to studies made by the *Max-Planck-Institut für ausländisches öffentliches Recht und Völkerrecht* (Beiträge zum ausländischen öffentlichen Recht und Völkerrecht, volume 44), and the Treaty. However, since he found the contested regulation to be legal there was no point in examining such problems as the *faute (Verschulden)*, the damage and the causal relation.

The Court accepted the reasoning by the Advocate-General insofar as the act should be illicit (*Unrechtmässig*) and added that the act would only incur liability if there was a sufficiently characterised breach of a superior rule of law protecting the individuals which had first to be examined; since the condition was not fulfilled the Court did not proceed into further examinations[9]. The Court expressed itself more clearly in the case of *CIE* (R.XVIII: 403) in consideration 1"la réparation du préjudice . . . causé par un comportement fautif de la Commission" or in the German original version "eines Anspruch auf Ersatz des Schadens, der ihnen durch, ein schuldhaftes Verhalten der Kommission". The Court continued (consideration 12) "aurait commis une illégalité engageant sa responsabilité; (attendu 13) que, s'agissant d'acts normatifs etc" and went on with an examination of such a violation. The outcome was the same as in the case of *Schöppenstedt,* since the contested acts were not considered illegal and the Court concluded that there was no point in examining the other conditions for responsibility due to an illegal behaviour.

From the cases of *Wünsche, Merkur, Werhahn, Holtz and Willemsen, Continentale and CNTA* one may perhaps draw the conclusion of a new development concerning the importance of the notion of the fault to community liability; this coincides with the enlargement of the Communities although the facts involved only in two cases are related to the time for the enlargement or after that event. One notes the following:

1) In the above-mentioned cases the Court has in its judgements not once mentioned the words *faute* or *faute de service;* the last time it did so was in the *CIE Case.*

2) A similar phrasing as employed in the case of *Lütticke* was resumed in the *Holtz & Willemsen Case,* (R.1974:694) i.e. that the following conditions at the same time should be present to incur liability, namely the illegal behaviour of an institution, a real damage and a causal connection between the behaviour and the alleged damage, whereafter the Court continued "que, s'agissant d'un acte normatif etc" but did not mention a fault or any culpability.

3) In the case of *Continentale* the Court took the view that the incomplete information delivered by the Council was of the nature to incur liability but without mentioning any *faute* or *faute de service* as it did in the *Temple Case* (R.IX:600, 601). The Advocate-General Trabucchi (p. 149) pointed out *that* the illicit action was constituted by the breach of the legitimate confidence of the merchants concerned and *that* the fault (*culpabilité*) was situated in the resolution taken without due diligence, and *that* the existence or the absence of an offence depended on whether the persons who normally follow the general obligation to inform themselves would have been enticed to commit error or not.

4) In the *CNTA Case* the Court found for the first time that a community institution had violated a superior rule of law incurring liability, through not having included transitional measures in a regulation for the protection of

71

certain merchants' legitimate confidence in community legislation.

5) In contrast to the Court the Advocates-General have in all these cases considered the *faute de service* as the basis for liability in which the illegality is the first element to be established.

In order to appreciate these elements one should in addition also note some other circumstances. All the cases mentioned but the *Continentale Case* have concerned illegalities in one form or the other in the context of normative acts where the illegality is related to special conditions. It is not sufficient that an illegality exists but it has to be evident i.e., a gross violation and violate a superior rule of law protecting the individuals[10] and consequently where the nonexistence of any illegality there is no practical need to continue further examinations of the case. These rules are aligned to the fact that the Council and the Commission concerning economic policy matters have a margin of discretionary power which only can be brought under legal control when committing material mistakes, evident errors or abuse of power, according to Advocate-General Mayras in the *Merkur Case,* (R.1973:1087; cf. art 33 (1) ECSC). Accordingly, there is a certain space for mistakes which will not incur liability "des considérations qui n'étaient pas manifestement erronées", *Merkur Case,* R.1973:1075, of which the limits are not distinct but subject to considerations. This is illustrated by the *Werhahn Case* in which the Court considered that an omission to act by the Council did not cause certain provisions to be illegal, whilst the Advocate-General Roemer considered the provisions to be illegal and thought the Council had committed a *grave erreur d'appréciation* in not taking any action (p. 1270). Concerning the Court's constant statement as to the liability for normative acts the Advocate-General interpreted in the *Merkur Case* (p. 1084) the critera as the mere gross violation of the rules protecting the individuals will incur liability, and the absence of such a violation makes it impossible to charge an institution with a *faute de service.*

This may mean, it is not necessary expressly to look for the fault (culpability) which thus is considered to be implied when this particular breach exists. This view is supported by the *CNTA Case* in which the Court established such a violation to exist and incur community liability but however without mentioning a fault or *faute de service*[11].

The constant omission by the Court during the last years to refer to the notion of *faute de service*—not only relating to normative acts but also concerning the general conduct of an institution (*Continentale Case*)—might indicate that the *faute de service* is given up as a point of reference although the appreciation *in concreto* of the prudence and diligence of an institution is implicitly retained[12]. The statement referred to above in the *Willemsen & Holtz Case* concerning the requirements for incurring liability appears to express only the basical elements of community liability which have to be further qualified and thus not exhaustively to regulate the question of fault. The Court did so as to illegal normative acts and the causal connection in the Schöppenstedt and Continentale Cases and the nature of the damage in the Kampffmeyer Case.

However, the position of faute de service is at present uncertain, and in substance the conclusions emerging from the Kampffmeyer Case, which dealt with an annulled decision as the basis for indemnity, have not yet been superseded.

Concerning the gravity of the fault it appears from the Kampffmeyer Case (R.XIII:340) that the Court rejected the Commission's allegation that the responsibility of administrative organs—according to general principles common to the laws of the Member-States—in charge of control only was incurred in cases of a faute lourde, but took the view that the Commission had to be as careful as the national authorities regardless of the nature of the powers devolving on the Commission from article 22 of the regulation concerned; the Commission assumed an independent liability for the maintenance of a safeguarding measure. However, one should not perhaps draw any general conclusions from the non-applicability of the degrees of fault in this case, but it would seem likely in general that the Court would put emphasis on that aspect in its considerations within the Treaties of Rome considering their multifarious activities compared with the limited ones of the ECSC Treaty.

Nor is there any case-law on faute personelle relating to the Treaties of Rome, and the Court seems in general to be reluctant to establish one, besides, concerning the ECSC Treaty, the importance of drawing the distinction between a faute de service has obviously diminished after the new wording of article 40 (2) of that Treaty implying that the Community assumes the liability for the servants in relation to the injured person. Thus one notes that in the case of Kergall (R.II:25) the responsible persons could be identified; this was also the situation in the case of Willame (R.XI:804) where the Commission had committed irregularities which were chiefly due to a high funcionary exceeding his powers and being ignorant of elementary provisions in the staff regulation; in the case of Feram (R.V:517) it was however not demonstrated that a faute personelle had been committed by an agent of the High Authority. The same policy of the Court seems in this respect to prevail concerning all three Treaties, and one may suppose that only when a fault is entirely related to a servant and that this is clearly evident, will Court establish the liability of the Community on the ground of faute personelle. Consequently, in practice, one does not meet with the co-existence of these two notions.

It is however, in principle, important to keep in mind the existence of three Treaties, with somewhat different aims and frameworks, and to point out that, on the one hand, it cannot be admissible to build one single system for the non-contractual liability of the Communities based on elements collected from the case-laws relating to the three Treaties, but, on the other hand, the fact is that the Treaties are administered by the same Court and the concept of European integration speaks in favour of a certain uniformity in this respect; therefore the adaptation of the conditions relating to each Treaty regarding the liability of the Communities is quite natural and also desirable, but the situation calls for precaution when drawning conclusions from the case-law of one Treaty in pretending to be applicable to another.

Finally, some remarks should be made concerning the particular situation relating to the civil servants of the Communities and their actions for indemnity. Some cases relating to the time before 1962 which was the year the staff regulations of the EEC and EAEC Treaties as well as of the ECSC Treaty came into force, reveal some specific information concerning the nature of the servants' actions for indemnity, since the Treaties contain only a few provisions directly applicable to the servants. It emerges from those cases that the provisions of the Treaties and their relating texts are only partly analogously applicable to the servants' actions. From the statements of the Advocate-General Roemer in the case of *Kergall* (R.II:38) it appears that concerning the legal control of a measure undertaken by an institution, the Court should be submitted to the same limits as in an action purporting directly to the annulment of the measure and thus excluding an examination of whether the measures are proper and suitable (see artt. 33 (1) and 36 of the ECSC Treaty). For the remaining part of the indemnity action, which is a *recours de pleine juridiction,* the Court should have the utmost amount of discretion of appreciation. However, legal control is not restricted to formal decisions coming under article 173 of the EEC Treaty but also other kinds of decisions due to article 179 may be included (*Lachmüller,* R.VI:969). From the *Bourgaux Case* (R.II:435) it would seem that almost all measures taken against the servants could be challenged in an action of annulment inspite of the rules of the Treaties which are normally applicable. Furthermore, the servants are also subjected to special provisions if such provisions have been incorporated into staff regulations or other relevant texts (see art. 42 of the ECSC Treaty and art. 179 of the EEC Treaty).

The servants' actions also provoke changes as to procedural rules, thus the Court rejected analogous applicability of the one month time limit provided for in articles 33 of the ECSC Treaty and 39 of the Statute of the Court in the case of *Mirossevich* (R.II:384). The same opinion was expressed in the case of *Lachmüller* (R.VI:970) in which the Advocate-General maintained that the time limit in article 173 EEC Treaty was not applicable to the servants' action (three months according to the Staff Regulation, art. 90) for annulment. One should also note the case of *Leda de Bruyn* (R.VIII:54) in which the Court considered the action to concern contractual liability and did not find the five years time limit expressed in article 43 of the Statute of the Court to be applicable, since that article concerned non-contractual liability. The basic and primary requirements of the indemnity action, the incriminating fact to which is attached a fault, the damage resulting from that fact and the causal connection between these two elements, apply to all actions for indemnity before the Court and are submitted to *pleine juridiction* regardless of the status of the plaintiff.

Footnotes chapter five

1. See for example to that end *Bürgerliches Gesetzbuch,* artt. 836 and 839 and *Grundgesetz* art. 34 which reads:
"Verletzt jemand in Ausübung eines ihm anvertrauten öffentlichen Amtes die ihm einem Dritten gegenüber obliegende Amtspflicht, so trifft die Verantwortlichkeit grundsätzlich den Staat oder die Körperschaft, in deren Dienst er steht. Bei Vorsatz oder grosser Fahrlässigkeit bleibt der Rückgriff vorbehalten. Für den Anspruch auf Schadensersatz und für den Rückgriff darf der ordentliche Rechtsweg nicht ausgeschlossen werden."

2. The Advocate-General Roemer said in the *Vloeberghs Case* (R.VII:469):
". . . le caractère illégal du comportement . . . ne suffit pas à fonder la responsabilité pour le préjudice invoqué. Il faut en outre prouver que cette attitude constitue une faute".

3. See W Much in *Der Haftung des Staates,* p. 747: "Wie oben dargelegt, beruht die Amtshaftung in den Gemeinschaften auf dem Verschuldenprinzip". Note also the declaration by L'Union Internationale des Magistrats, art. 8, Sixth Session in 1967 referred by F Dumon in *Cahiers de Droit Européen 1969,* p. 8:
". . . la faute consiste en un comportement s'écartant de la perspicacité ou de la prudence exigée pour le bon fonctionnement d'un service public".

The emphasis on the *in concreto* appreciation is further shown by *inter alia* the cases of *Meroni* (R.VII:377): ". . . du caractère complexe des éléments à prendre en considération" and of *Espérance-Longdoz* (R.XI:1344): ". . . dans ces conditions, la défenderesse s'étant trouvée dans l'impossibilité d'apprécier tous les éléments de la cause, on ne saurait lui reprocher de ne pas avoir pris d'initiative en vue d'éviter à la requérante l'erreur alléguée par celle-ci".

4. See Waline, *Traité Droit administratif,* p. 719: ". . . la responsabilité n'est pas engagé s'il apparait que la décision annulée pour vice de forme, était au fond justifiée; ou si l'autorité administratif avait un pouvoir discrétionaire de sort que le requérant ne peut justifier que l'autorisation aurait été accordée si la procédure regulière avait été observée; ou enfin si administration avait compétence liée".

See for comparative considerations relating to state liability of illegal concrete acts, P Germer in *Juristen,* 1967, pp. 449—463.

5. The wording in article 34 is according to M Lagrange simply a restatement of the ordinary "common law" provisions of article 40, *CML Review 1965/66,* p. 27.

6. Note that the text of the Treaty was changed on German initiative from reading *faute lourde* to its present wording on the very day before the Treaty was signed, W Much, *Amtshaftung im Recht der Europäischen Gemeinschaft für Kohle und Stahl,* p. 62 f.

7. See the declaration of *l'Union international des Magistrats,* article 8 (Dumon):
"La notion de faute citée expressément par l'article 40 CECA et incluse dans les art. 215, al. 2 CEE, et 188, al. 2 CEEA, doit, dans l'intéret de l'unité du droit communautaire et la sécurité juridique recevoir une interprétation uniforme dans l'application de ces trois dispositions".

8. See comments by L Goffin on the *Kampffmeyer Case* in *Cahiers 1968,* p. 82 f.

9. Cf. L Goffin and M Mahieu in *Cahiers 1972,* p. 688 who considered, "le caractère illicite de l'acte" to mean the fault.

10. According to Advocate-General Reischl (*Holtz & Willemsen Case,* R.1974:701) the expression
"violation suffisamment caractérisée d'un règle de protection de rang supérieur"

means simply the requirement of a
"violation *flagrante* de règles de droit".

11. The Advocate-General Roemer has separately treated (see the *Werhahn and Schöppenstedt Cases*) the illegality from the question of fault and made the remark in the former case (p. 1269):
"D'après les règles en matière de responsabilité non contractuelle (telles qu'elle ont été réspectées jusqu' à présent), à la constatation de l'illégalité doit faire suite l'examen de la question de savoir s'il y a faute".

In the *Schöppenstedt Case* the Court stated that the contested act at least should be illicit in order to incur liability which was interpreted by Goffin and Mahieu in *Cahiers 1972,* p. 688, to mean the fault. They also thought that the actual analysis by the Court purported to establish whether the Council had committed a fault or not in adopting the contested regulation. The Court concluded after the examination of the alleged violation that the specific violation relating to normative acts did not exist; the contested regulation was not found to be illegal.

H Schermers pronounced in *Legal issues of European integration 1975/1,* p. 127, concerning "wrongful legislation" that the Court does not review the legality of normative acts according to the grounds of article 173 but merely looks at the formula whether a superior rule of law protecting individuals has been violated. This seems not to be quite true, since one of the bases of article 173 is the infringement of the Treaty or any rule relating to its application, which not only covers but is the very basis for the specific rule of law mentioned. Furthermore, nothing seems to prevent a plaintiff from invoking any grounds for illegality if he thinks this will satisfy the mentioned requirements for incurring liability. It is more adequate to consider any illegal behaviour of an institution susceptible to incur liability but relating to normative acts the requirements have been qualified in a specific way limiting the actual number of acts incurring liability.

12. See *Merkur Case,* p. 1075, *Werhahn Case,* p. 1251, and *Willemsen & Holtz Case,* p. 697.

Chapter six

Additional requirements for rendering liability

§ 6.1 The relationship between articles 34 and 40 of the ECSC Treaty[1]

It follows from the first sentence of article 40 (1) that these two articles are related to each other and that there is an interplay with respect to both material matters as well as procedural ones[2]. It is suitable to distinguish between two categories of plaintiffs: 1) enterprises entitled to actions pursuant to article 33 and 2) persons who are not entitled to such actions (see the definition of the entitled persons in article 80) and to penetrate their different positions. For the former group the situation appears as follows.

An entitled undertaking may according to the conditions in article 33 or 35 contest a decision taken by the High Authority[3]. If the Court finds the contested act to be illegal, it will annul the act and refer the matter back to the High Authority. The plaintiff may at the same time ask the Court to declare that the annulled act involves a fault of such a nature as to incur the Community's liability. If the damage occurs after a successful action for annulment the plaintiff must be able to bring a separate action at a later date but within the time of preclusion allowed in accordance with article 40 of the Statute of the Court (ECSC). In such a case he probably could not refer to article 40 (1), since it would deprive the High Authority of its possibility to use its power in making good the harm suffered, but the plaintiff has to continue the interrupted procedure of article 34.

If the Court finds the contested decision to be legal, it is of course impossible to declare that it involves a fault rendering the liability, see the case of *Bergau*, R.VI:1015 and also *Leroy*[4]. If the act has been annulled the Court will declare at least on the demand of the plaintiff that it involves a fault incurring liability to the extent that the illegality could have been avoided by a good administration taking the specific circumstances of the case into consideration. Even though the mistake might have been avoided by a good administration one can imagine cases where liability is excluded. Thus at the violation of procedural rules a reparation generally seems to be excluded, especially if the rest of the act is in conformity with community law and if the High

Authority is able to take a new decision observing the procedural rules. However, the High Authority may not in general make a decision with retroactive effects and accordingly there may be cases where a reparation may take place.

If the High Authority fails in its obligations pursuant to article 34 (1), an action for indemnity may be brough before the Court (art. 34 (2)). However, the failure by the High Authority may comprise an illegal decision, and the only thing the plaintiff can do is to give the Court the opportunity to review the whole situation by bringing two actions: one for the indemnity according to article 34 (2) and one for annulment pursuant to article 33 or 35 to which the conditions in article 34 (1) apply for the possibilities of indemnity; by virtue of article 34 (2) the Court seems to have been endowed with the power to settle once and for all the question of the indemnity.

However, article 34 can be closed to the entitled enterprises for different reasons. Three main situations are distinguished:
1) an enterprise has omitted to introduce an action for annulment within the stipulated period of time
   a) although the damage appeared within the one month time limit,
   b) the damage was not foreseeable and occurred after the time limit;
2) an enterprise has no right to contest acts other than decisions or recommendations concerning it which are individual in character or general decisions or recommendations involving a misuse of power affecting it;
3) the Court is not allowed to consider certain points of views in judging the illegality (art. 33 (1)):
   "Toutefois, l'examen de la Cour ne peut porter sur l'appréciation de la situation découlant des faits ou circonstances économiques au vu de laquelle sont intervenues lesdites décisions ou recommendations, sauf s'il est fait grief à la Haute Autorité d'avoir commis un détournement de pouvoir ou d'avoir méconnu d'une manière patente les dispositions du traité ou toute règle de droit relative à son application" which means that the Court with the exclusion of such elements may find the act legal. This will apply to all circumstances.

It seems quite clear that an undertaking must exhaust the possibilities in article 34 before referring to article 40, but when the former cannot be used for an action the question arises to what extent can the latter article be used in seeking indemnity. In this context one should keep in mind that an action for annulment and an action for indemnity are two completely different things with respect to their aims and effects where the former purports to the suppression of a certain measure while the latter only aims at the reparation of the damage caused by a bad action[5].

Point 1) mainly poses the question of whether a non-annulled (illegal) act[6] may form the basis for an action of indemnity according to article 40. In the *Vloeberghs Case* (R.VII:424f) the Court did not find it necessary to make a pronouncement concerning a concrete act but found the alleged violation of the Treaty by the High Authority to be inherent in its lack of action, and this could be invoked as the basis of an action pursuant to article 40; note the plaintiff was not an enterprise entitled to actions pursuant to article 34[7]. Confer the case of *Kergall* where the Court found an illegal decision (non-annulled) —involving a fault rendering the liability—to be grounds for an action for indemnity.

In the *Meroni Case* (R.VII:334) the Court stated that the dispute in question should be judged only upon the basis of article 40 and that "... il convient d'écarter d'emblée le problème de la légalité ou de l'illégalité des décisions par lesquelles le système de péréquation a été créé et modifié, et de rechercher uniquement si la gestion du mécanisme financier relève une faute de service imputable à la défenderesse". The decision of delegation of power by the High Authority and the defects inherent in the general decisions relating to the equalisation system of scrap iron were not to be examined in the present case based on article 40. The extent of these statements seems to be unclear; one should note *that* the plaintiffs had invoked a *faute de service* and that the Court concluded article 40, *that* the plaintiffs were enterprises entitled to an action pursuant to article 34 and *that* the plaintiffs alleged that the committed *faute de service* consisted of the non-notification within due time by the High Autority to the plaintiffs of their amounts of contributions to the equalisation system i.e. the execution of the system. The Advocate-General Lagrange took the view (p. 349) that article 34 was applicable to the decisions declared "illégales par voie d'exception" in the case of *Meroni* (R.IV:14) where the Court annulled some individual decisions based on those general decisions[8]. He examined whether the conditions for indemnity according to article 34 were fulfilled concerning the decision of delegation of power and found the answer to be negative, whereas there was no special damage caused. Furthermore, he did not find any fault on the part of the High Authority with respect to the execution of the system. It seems that the Court had only looked to the conduct of the High Authority relating to the notification and dismissed the arguments drawn from the illegality of the general decisions, since the plaintiffs had the possibility to rely upon the remedies offered in article 34 to that end.

Article 34 and 40 (1) should probably not be read in such a manner that illegalities manifested by concrete acts or implied decisions are generally regulated in article 34, while article 40 only concerns other kinds of mistakes made by the institutions, but article 34 should exhaustively regulate a specific situation i.e. indemnity matters brought by certain undertakings and their associations in the context of annulled decisions. The enterprises which are submitted to the Treaty have to refer in the first instance to article 34 for seeking indemnity from annulled acts, but otherwise the general scope of application of article 40 (1) is not explicit from the article itself but is left to the Court to determine.

Even though the Court has not yet pronounced itself in a clear way on this matter, one may perhaps believe that the Court would accept in certain situations an action for indemnity based on article 40 by invoking the illegality of a non-annulled act and the fault attached to it in constituting a *faute de service,* where the establishment of the illegality pursuant to article 33 in itself is only an incidental matter in the action for indemnity.

There seems to be no general reason for admitting actions under article 40 belonging to the category in 1a) also including implied decisions[9]; however, one can imagine two exceptions: article 39 (3) of the Statute of the Court (*force majeure*) is applicable, and where an omission by the High Authority one may think of situations in which an annulment cannot be required (see the Advocate-General in the *Vloeberghs Case,* p. 448), whereby it should be possible to lodge an action, although in general actions should be possible in situations under 1b).

The admissibility advocated to actions in situations under 1) based on article 40 involves the same acts which might have been challenged, annulled and provoked indemnity according to article 34 but cases under 2) concern acts which the undertakings are not allowed to contest according to article 33 (2). The question is here whether every possibility to claim damage from an alleged illegality on the basis of article 40 is excluded [10]. Such a possibility would mainly concern the situation in which a general decision cannot be contested by means of misuse of power affecting the undertaking or there is no individual decision following to which article 36 can be applied. On the one hand, one could argue that there would be no remedies against a number of acts performed in the implementation of the Treaty which thereby also being excluded from the jurisdiction of national courts, and on the other hand, that article 34 purported to limit the liability of the Community with a view to easing the financial burden finally incumbent upon the undertakings themselves, and besides general decisions normally cause a general damage affecting all undertakings. Perhaps a solution would be formally to allow the action but to apply the requisite of a direct and special damage which would cause most such actions to fail on their merits. Furthermore, such an action would normally only be subsidiary to actions under article 34.

Third parties to the Treaty must necessarily follow article 40 (see, *Vloeberghs Case,* R.VII:426 *in fine* and the *Algera Case,* R.III:86). The question is whether they should be permitted to invoke also concrete illegal acts in an action for indemnity; the answer seems to be in the affirmative (see *Vloeberghs Case,* R.VII:450 and 453) since another solution would be unjustified and detrimental to the legal security of the Treaty, which is normally a chief concern of the Court. However, it is justified to ask what limitations would be added to the action concerning for example the nature of the acts to be contested and the damage; see further below §§ 6.3 and 7.1.

§ 6.2 The relationship between actions for annulment and indemnity in the Treaties of Rome[11]

The persons entitled to challenge an act in an action for annulment are restricted as appears from article 173. However, according to article 184 anyone may invoke the illegality of an regulation by means of *illegality with exception* in any action where the legality is in question. The problems is on what terms the illegality may be invoked as a prerequistie in an action for indemnity and in particular where the situation of the plaintiff after an action for indemnity will be identical or similar to the result of an action of annulment of the same contested act. Both actions are evidently a legal control but their aims and consequences are different. To some extent these questions are similar to the situations already discussed above in § 6.1 though concerning articles 34 and 40 of the ECSC Treaty; the Court has so far not expressed itself in a clear and comprehensive manner which accordingly leaves them open to speculation. The views expressed by the Court relating to the Rome Treaties are much clearer and may exercise an influence on the approach under the ECSC Treaty.

One should note that according to article 175 of the EEC Treaty the failure to act and the undefined position after a calling upon the institution to do so does not imply a decision which is susceptible to challenge in an action of annulment as in the ECSC Treaty pursuant to article 35 (3) but purports to the establishment of an infringement (see § 2.1, notes 5 and 6); therefore there will be no annulment but an infringement censured by the Court (see the statement of Advocate-General in the *CIE Case*, R. XVIII:416). The persons entitled to such an action are restricted in the same way as in article 173. Also after the establishment of an infringement in such a way there may be the possibility of compensation; persons not entitled to such an action may invoke the infringement by omission as a preliminary matter in an action for indemnity, see e.g. the *Lütticke Case*.

Also here as in § 6.1 it is suitable to distinguish between two categories of plaintiffs: I. those entitled to lodge an action for annulment and II. those not entitled, and to consider their possibilities to lodge various actions.

I. Entitled to an action of annulment of a certain act:

a) An action brought within the time limit and supplemented by one for indemnity based on the illegality of the contested act
   1. The act is annulled and the institution has to comply with the judgement according to article 176 (1) which does not, according to the same article second paragraph, exclude the possibility of claiming indemnity according to article 215 (2); see the case of *Lasalle,* R.X:57 and the statement by the Advocate-General Roemer in the *Plaumann*

Case, R.IX:245. The indemnity action can apparently also be lodged in a separate action at a later date after the annulment but within the period of limitation, see the cases of *Toepfer,* and *Kampffmeyer* and *Becker.*

2. The act is not annulled since the act is found to be legal which means that the action for indemnity is declared to be unfounded by the Court; see for example the cases of *Fonzi,* R.XI:616 and *Fux,* R.XV:145 which also included subsidiary actions for indemnity not based on the illegality of the contested acts but on other grounds—which moreover, were not well-founded. Many actions of annulment have been supplemented by a subsidiary action for indemnity in case the principal action of annulment should fail where the indemnity action has been based on facts other than the illegality of the contested act which have been admissible.

b) An action of annulment not brought within the required time limit but instead after that time one of indemnity

1. Because the plaintiff has omitted to bring forward an action for annulment. It follows from the case of *Collignon,* R.XIII:470 that one cannot compensate for failure to adhere to the rules of procedure in such an action by lodging an action for indemnity; note also that the action for indemnity in the case of *Schreckenberg,* (R.XII:796f) was considered to be a disguised action for annulment and dismissed as inadmissible. This is a notion that exists in national laws of the Member-States. The same applied in the *Schots-Kortner Case* (R.1974:188, considerations 7—10).

2. The plaintiff has omitted to bring an action for annulment because the damage resulting from the act occurred after the expiry of the two months limitation which also raises the question of disguised action of annulment. Concerning the admissibility of this action, see below under II.

c) An action for annulment may be inadmissible on bases other than those mentioned under b 1) because there is no decision to annul or the contested measure is not susceptible to form an action; however those measures can be elements in an action for indemnity based on mistakes other than illegal decisions, see *Labeyrie,* R.XIV:432.

II. Not entitled to an action for annulment of a certain act:

The Commission had put forward the theory in the *Lütticke Case* that an action for indemnity based on a non-censured illegality should be inadmissible since in reality it was a disguised action of *carence* and achieved the same or similar results as such an action, to which the plaintiff was not permitted. However, the Court dismissed this approach (page 337):

"attendu que le recours en indemnité des articles 178 et 215, alinéa 2, a été institué par le traité comme une voie de recours autonome, ayant sa fonction particulière dans le cadre du système des voies de recours et subordonnée à des conditions d'exercice concues en vue de son objet spécifique;

qu'il serait contraire à cette autonomie du recours, autant qu'à l'efficacité du système général des voies de droit instituées par le traité, de considérer comme cause d'irrecevabilité le fait que, dans certaines circonstances, l'exercice du recours en indemnité pourrait conduire à un résultat comparable à celui du recours en carence institué par l'article 175".

This implies the incidental recognition of the illegality by omission but does not oblige the institution to take the measures provide for in article 176 (1). In the cases of *Schöppenstedt* and *CIE,* the Council and the Commission took the view that the actions for indemnity did not aim at compensating the damage resulting from their faults but at suppressing the judicial effects of the contested acts. The Court announced the same as above but substituted the last quoted section by (see page 984 and 404 respectively): "qu'elle se différencie du recours en annulation en ce qu'elle tend, non à la suppression d'une mésure déterminée, mais à la réparation du préjudice causé par une institution dans l'exercice de ses fonctions" and added: "que les recours en réparation visent seulement à la reconnaissance d'un droit à réparation et, par conséquent, à une prestation destinée à produire ses effets uniquement à l'égard des requérants". This seems to be quite compréhensible and justifiable, since in these cases[12] the plaintiffs had not been permitted according to articles 173 and 175 to obtain the establishment of the alleged illegalities and thus were unable to attain compensation for damage which had eventually been suffered. Only if someone else, by chance from the view of the plaintiffs, had been successful in establishing the illegality, it had been possible for the plaintiffs to invoke the illegalities.

The *Plaumann Case* caused discussion at the time when it was delivered by the Court[13] by appearing not to be based on principles belonging to the laws of the Member-States insofar as the Court stated after having found the action for indemnity to be admissible and in judging its substance that:

"il y a lieu de constater que le préjudice allégué par le requérant est basé sur cette décision (which he was not allowed to challenge in an action for annulment), et que le recours en indemnité vise en réalité le retrait des effets juridiques que la décision litigieuse a comportés pour le requérant; attendu qu'en l'espèce la décision attaquée n'a pas été annulée; qu'un acte administratif non annulé ne saurait etre en lui-meme constitutif d'une faute lésant les administrés; que ceux-ci ne sauraient donc prétendre à des dommage-intéret du fait de cet acte".

Concerning the latter part dealing with the annulment, it appears from the cases mentioned above that it is not necessary for the act, alleged to have caused the damage, to be annulled or censured[14], but the first part compared with the one cited from the cases of *Schöppenstedt* and *CIE* raises the problem of a disguised action for annulment. In the case of *CIE* the problem was salient insofar as the plaintiff had previously brought an action for annulment, which had been rejected as inadmissible, directed against the same provision which was alleged to be illegal in the action for indemnity and generating the damage, but yet the Court upheld the earlier statements concerning the autonomy of the action for indemnity.

According to the Advocate-General Dutheillet de Lamothe in the *CIE Case* (R.XVIII:412 f), articles 177 and 184 only aimed at the establishment of the indivudual rights (*droits subjectifs*) of the plaintiff which the combination of articles 178 and 215 (2) also did, this would not mean an evasion of article 173 (2)[15]. The motives for the restriction in this paragraph were partly, the effects *erga omnes* and partly, the retroactive effects of a declared annulment; those effects did not occur from the establishment of a subjective right relating to the plaintiff. The Advocate-General Hanry Mayras took the same views in the *Merkur Case* (R.1973:1079). However, considering the cases of *Plaumann, Collignon* and *Schreckenberg* the attention is drawn to the specific *intention* of the plaintiff by his action whether he was aiming at the *suppression* of a certain measure and if that fact should constitute a qualification of the substantial nature of the indemnity action as such, and whether, if having the purpose of suppression, even if only with effects towards the plaintiff, it would be inadmissible.

This problem was solved in the case of *Merkur* (R.1973:1015) where the Commission doubted that an action for indemnity based on the illegality of a community regulation could be admissible, where it intended to obtain an identical or comparable pecuniary result to such a one emerging from an annulment of the regulation concerned, which the plaintiff was not allowed to challenge. The Court answered by repeating its earlier statement in the *Schöppenstedt* and *CIE Cases* "que le recours en indemnité vise seulement à la reconnaissance d'un droit à réparation et, par conséquence, à une prestation destinée à produire ses effets uniquement à l'égard du requérant".

Through this statement of the Court one may consider the situation to have been clarified, i.e. the intention is of no importance and the indemnity action assumes its own character and field of application not mixed with but separated from the action for annulment, and thus the *Plaumann Case* appears accordingly as being superseded also in that respect. But nevertheless the Council once more made the objection in the case of *Holtz &*

Willemsen (R.1974:681) that the action by the plaintiff was inadmissible, since it in reality aimed at modifications or completions of a regulation which the plaintiff could not contest, neither according to article 173 nor article 175. The Court, however, maintained its earlier views in reiterating the caracteristics of the action for indemnity.

In the context of preliminary rulings pursuant to article 177 of the EEC Treaty the legality of community acts may be contested by a plaintiff involved in an action before a national court. This procedure was envisaged by the Commission in the *Merkur Case* (R.1973:1069) which caused the Advocate-General strongly to criticise (p. 1080) the Court's judgement in the case of *Haegeman* (R.1972:1005) in which the Court had primarily referred the plaintiff to national jurisdiction in seeking indemnity. Even if the statements by the Court do not appear as clear, this case of Haegeman seems to be special all the more so, since the Court declared in the case of *Merkur*: "la Cour a été saisie dans le cadre de sa compétence et qu'elle est, dès lors, tenue d'examiner si ces règlements sont ou non entachés des irrégularités invoquées", since it would otherwise have been contrary to a good legal order and economy in procedure, if the plaintiff had been compelled to adopt the lengthy procedure of referring himself first to the national authorities in order to obtain recognitition of the illegality, after which the foreclosure in article 43 of the Statutes of the Court mostly would apply. It took Haegeman two and a half year by means of a preliminary ruling from the Court to obtain the answer to the question as to the legality of the contested levy (R.1974:449). However, this case does not appear as a breach of the line followed from the *Lütticke Case* but rather as an exception due to the specific circumstances in this case[16].

Moreover, the cases under 2b) above would then be admissible, which seems quite natural since one cannot blame the injured person because the damage did not occur or was not known to him within the time limitation for an action, but on the other hand, the cases of *Collignon* and *Schreckenberg* still show that one cannot use an action for indemnity as a substitute for an action of annulment which the plaintiff has been allowed to lodge but which for some reason has failed.

§ 6.3 Violation of a rule destined to protect the interests of the plaintiff

The requisite that the violated rule must be destined to protect the interest of the plaintiff (*Schutznormstheorie*) was advanced for the first time in the case of *Vloeberghs* (R.VII:430f):

"ce n'est pas la requérante qui pourrait demander réparation pour une prétendue lésion de ses droits qu'aurait entrainée le défaut d'action de la Haute Autorité".

One notes from the comments upon this case by Advocate-General Lagrange[17] that he distinguished between a breach of a subjective right constituted by a *faute de service,* damage and a causal relationship between them and a legitimate interest. However, the plaintiff in the case of *Vloeberghs* could not show that his interests were lawfully protected and constituted a proper right of his, since the principle of free movement of goods only was created for the Member-States and the enterprises subjected to the Treaty concerning community goods. The field of application of this rule is not certain; perhaps it only applies to third parties of the Treaty (see R.VII:430). Furthermore, he said, that one could see from this case how subtle the distinction was between these two kinds of interests which is indeed very true[18]. The notion was resumed in the cases of *Kampffmeyer* and *Becker.* The Court pronounced that the aims of the regulation concerned were to ensure support of the agricultural market and progressively set up a common market with free circulation of the goods concerned which was a general interest, but the interest of the producers and persons affected by the free trade between the Member-States had been expressly mentioned in the considerations of the regulation, and as article 22 was an exception from the general rule, this article also concerned the same interest. Even though dealing with such a general interest one could not exclude that the plaintiffs were englobed considering their activities on the agricultural market, and

"si l'application des règles de droit dont il s'agit n'est pas en général de nature à concerner directement et individuelement lesdites entreprises, cela n'empeche que la protection de leurs intérets peut etre et, dans l'éspece, est en effet visée par ces règles de droit; que l'argument de la défenderesse. . . l'article 22 du règlement ne vise pas la protection des intérets des requérantes, ne peut dont etre retenu".

The plaintiffs had taken the view that since the Court had recognised the annulled decision as *concerning them directly and individually* they could also ask for indemnity pursuant to article 215 (2). This was as such supported by the Advocate-General who also pointed out that one should not confuse the conditions concerning the admissibility to an action of annulment with the rules concerning those of a well-founded action for indemnity; however, he thought that the Court also should be liberal here as it had been concerning the access to the annulment in judging the action of indemnity. A liberal view was also said to prevail in Germany concerning the application of the rule (applied in a way *très souple*) being the country from which the notion mainly originated, article 34 of the Constitution[19].

The principle has furthermore been repeated in the *Schöppenstedt Case* and subsequent cases dealing with normative acts involving choices of economic policies[20] where a serious breach of a superior rule of law protecting the individuals shall exist to incur liability. The question is, which are the rules of law being superior in character and also protecting the interests of the individuals. Concerning *a superior rule of law,* it appears from the case-law that such a rule may be found among basic principles established for a certain activity; in most cases such rules will be found in the Treaty and equal texts but also in a *règlement de base* for an activity. To these rules must also be added following from article 173 "violation of the treaty or any rule of law relating to its application", rules of law relating to human rights, which emerges from the *Internationale Handelsgesellschaft Case* (R.XVI:1125) and other fundamental principles of law; see the CNTA Case[21].

The criteria of the protection of individuals has not yet been sufficently defined. Goffin wrote in *Cahiers 1972,* page 689, concerning the *Schöppenstedt Case* that the Court did not look for whether the allegedly violated rules had the object of protecting the individuals although this seemed to be the case concerning the rules in question. He thought that the concept should not be too narrow and added:

"elle (the Court) énonce uniquement que la règle violée doit protéger les particuliers, sans autre précision. On observera qu'ainsi formulée, la condition perd une grande part de sa signification. La violation d'une règle ne protégeant pas les particuliers, par exemple une règle de forme ou une règle d'organisation des Communautés, ne parait pas pouvoir constituer la *cause* d'un préjudice allégué par un particulier. Il suffirait donc de placer le problème sur le plan du lien de causalité. La référence à la *Schutznormstheorie* deviendrait ainsi inutile".

Schermers, on the other hand, *opus cited,* page 127, has the opinion that the Court is primarily concerned with the protection of vested rights and stated: "The formula employed is broad. It is not limited to normative rules *specifically intended* for the protection of the *interests of the claimant,* but accepts any serious breach of any major rule of law which in general protects individuals"; this seems to be sustained by the *CNTA Case.*

In the *Lütticke Case* the Advocate-General Dutheillet de Lamothe discussed this principle, but the Court did not mention it although it commented on the criteria for community liability. The question which arises from this silence is whether the plaintiff satisfied the principle or whether it was not applicable in this case. In the similar case of *Vloeberghs* the Court directly proceeded to examine whether any protected interest of the plaintiff had been violated before examining the violation as such, whilst in the *Lütticke Case* it started to examine the alleged violation. Since it is logical firstly to examine whether the plaintiff may invoke the alleged violation or not, one might conclude that the requisite was applicable and fullfilled in this case, although the Advocate-General did not think so as to the latter aspect, who primarily examined this question[22].

One notes, however, that all these cases, in which the principle has been resumed, have concerned concrete illegal acts or illegalities by omission, therefore it is possible to presume that such cases require this additional qualification. It then depends on the rigidity with which the Court employs the criteria as to what effects it will have on the actual possibilities for obtaining compensation for suffered damage.

§ 6.4 Some procedural matters

For a general outline of the procedure before the Court see Chapter two, here it shall however only be dealt with some specific matters relating to actions for indemnity.

Articles 40, 43 and 44 of the Statutes of the Court of the ECSC, EEC and EAEC Treaties respectively are almost identical, and establish the rule that proceedings for indemnity must be instituted before the expiry of five years calculated from the occurrence of the fact alleged to have caused the damage. This period can be interrupted by the institution of court proceedings or by request to the institution concerned. In the latter event proceedings must be instituted within two months before the Court. However, the second and the third sentences of these articles have appeared with respect to the prior application made to an institution as not being clear in their meaning regarding the preclusion. The Court clarified this item in the *Kampffmeyer Case* (R.XIII:337), inasmuch as such a reclamation did not cut short the period of limitation but purported to protect the interested party. The third sentence had merely the purpose of delaying the expiration of the five years limitation when a request had been made to the institution concerned, which would implicitly mean that a demand to an institution does not start another period of five years (see Advocate-General Gand, page 349f.

In the case of *CIE* the plaintiffs had sent the Commission letters asking for recognition of their rights for indemnity which the Commission refused in letters addressed three months later to the plaintiffs, who in their actions before the Court asked for the annulment of the implied decision dismissing their requests which the letters had confirmed. However, the Court held these actions to have the same aim as the actions based on article 215 (2) and could therefore not be of any interest to the plaintiffs and were therefore rejected as inadmissible. The Advocate-General Dutheillet de Lamothe concluded (page 415) that contrary to the procedure in certain national laws, article 215 did not impose the obligation of an administrative reclamation to a community institution prior to an action for indemnity before the Court but that such a measure was voluntary.

Concerning the matter of proof in the proceedings before the Court one bears in mind that in indemnity cases the Court has *pleine juridiction* or *unbe-*

schränkter Rechtssprechungsbefugnis when once the illegality is establish and is additionally guided by the *investigation (Meroni Case,* R.VII:319) and negotiations *(Laminoirs Case,* R.XI:1153) maxims (artt. 45 (2) and 60 and 40 (1) respectively of the Rules of Procedure). In article 38 (1) of the Rules of Procedure it is laid down the qualities of the written application which i.a. shall contain a brief summary of the grounds of the action and the offers of proof. The Court stated in the case of *Meroni* (R.VII:340) that the injured person had to offer at least *le commencement de la preuve* or *Beweiseintritt (n'ont ni preuve, ni offert de prouver, Five Lille Case,* R.VII:593 and *CIE Case,* R.XVIII:408) which was also the view of the Advocate-General Roemer (*Vloeberghs Case,* R.VII:477 and *Schöppenstedt Case,* R.XVII:1002) who expressly stated that the burden of proof is in principle incumbent on the injured person[23]. It is thus not sufficient to

"borne à declarer. . . mais elle n'a pas fait état d'aucun élément de natur à établir. . ." (R.XVII:1002).

However, the burden of proof on the injured party is only true to a certain point, since the Court does not impose an unrealistic burden, which appears from the *Kampffmeyer Case* (R.XIII:342, 343).

In French law it is up to the injured person to show there is fault on the part of the administration but in certain instances the burden of proof is reversed insofar that the administration may exonerate itself from a presumed fault. If the link of cause between a damage and the action by the administration which is alleged to have caused the damage is established, the *Conseil d'État* in France has concluded that a defective functioning of the administration [24] may be presumed, which seems to have been a method also used by the Court when it has not been convinced of the existence of a *faute de service.* In some cases the Court has proceeded to examine the existence of a damage (see the cases of *Meroni,* R.VII:325, *Feram,* R.XI:402, *Modena,* R.X:419, *Hainaute-Sambre,* R.XI:1364 and *Chatillon,* R.XII:266) and where the existence of a probable damage it has continued to examine the causal connection (see the cases of *Temple,* R.IX:589 and *Worms,* R.VIII:401).

Concerning the civil servants' actions, the Court seems to have been less exigent compared to cases involving other parties, see for example the cases of *Fiddelaar* (R.VI:1119) and *Richez-Parise* (R.XVI:325).

Footnotes chapter six

1. On this matter see *inter alia* articles by L Cartou, J Blanchet and R Knöpfle in *Kölner Schriften zum Europarecht,* p. 323 f. See also *Knöpfle in NJW 1961,* p. 2287. One notes however, that the views on this matter in the doctrine quite often differ.

2. See W Much in *Haftung des Staates*, p. 746 f and L Goffin and M Mahieu in *Cahiers 1972*, p. 70 f.

3. Note, article 35 means inertia by the High Authority, see further footnote 6 in § 2.1.

4. Cf. for example the case of *Five Lille Cail* (R.VII:517) where the plaintiff had sought annulment of a decision and subsidiarily brought an action for indemnity according to article 40. The first action was rejected but the second founded; one should note that the actions for annulment and indemnity relied upon different bases.

5. See the *Vloeberghs Case*, R.VII:424 and 426.

6. See Goffin in *CML Review 1963/64*, p. 357, from which it appears that at least in Belgium, France and Germany there exist no rules providing for the annulment of an act as a prerequisite in an action for indemnity caused by that illegal act; see also the Advocate-General Roemer in the case of *Toepfer*, R.XI:565.

7. The Advocate-General Roemer thought in this case (R.VII:450) that a third party to the Treaty could invoke article 40 in order to have the legality of a decision examined by the Court.

8. Article 36 (3) was in that case not considered as a special provision with a limited scope of applicability but as a general principle "dont l'article 36 prévoit l'application au cas particulier d'un recours de pleine juridiction", p. 26 f.

9. See further below § 6.2 on the competition between actions for annulment and indemnity. Note, however, the case of *Collignon* where it was impossible to repair the omission of introduction of an action for annulment by an action for indemnity, R.XIII:480.

10. Both W Much, *Die Amtshaftung im Recht der Europäischen Gemeinschaft für Kohle und Stahl*, p. 61 and L Goffin, *Journal des Tribunaux 1963*, p. 116, consider such a right to be excluded. J Blanchet, *opus.cited*, p. 349 thinks that the *Vloeberghs Case* indicates the wish not to exclude all rights of the victim to obtain reparation for caused damage by the Commission in such a situation.

11. See H. Schermers *opus cited* pp. 121—126, and L Goffin and M Mahieu in *Cahiers 1972*, pp. 69—76.

12. In the case of *Wünsche* the defendant did not contest the admissibility of the action of indemnity in this sense.

13. See *inter alia* the Advocate-General Roemer in the *Toepfer Case*, R.XI:565 and L Goffin, *CML Review 1963/64*.

14. See the Advocate-General Roemer in the case of *CIE* (R.XVII:991 f); see also L Goffin and M Mahieu in *Cahiers 1972*, pp. 67—80 and 680 f.

15. Note also that article 177 may result in an appreciation by the Court of the legality of an act, but before an action of indemnity could be brought before the Court on the basis of the so established illegality, the expiry of the time limit in article 43 of the Statute of the Court may have ended.

16. One notes in particular from that case that, the claims for the inapplicability of the Commission's regulations, exemption, annulment of the individual decision, purported according to the Advocate-General by means of article 184 to modify articles in the basic regulation of the Council, and that the restitution evidently belonged to the national jurisdiction. The claim for indemnity was based on mistakes committed

by the Commission in its implementing measures of the Council regulation. The indemnity action is not clear, and the Court's statement does not bring any further clarity, and it is hard to see how the community liability should depend on the legality of the collection of the tax which belonged to national authorities.

17. *CMLReview 1965/66,* p. 25 f. Cf. L Goffin in *Droit des Communautés Européennes,* p. 150, where he considered this rule to create a discriminatory limitation which was not justified.

18. One notes from Belgian law, P Wigny, *Droit Administratif,* p. 294 f that state liability requires *inter alia* "la lésion d'un droit". The damage is not considered to be enough but the interests of the injured person must be legally protected, where article 1382 of *Code de Civil* has a certain field of application but additionally the individuals also have a legal interest in the lawful functioning of the public services which is laid down with respect to each service, and this *Loi du service public* creates obligations on behalf of the administrations.

19. L Goffin expressed the view in *Cahiers 1968,* p. 88 that this rule was an unnecessary complication and asked the question if it was not reasonable to recognise that the administrated had a general right to expect a lawful conduct by the authorities. Furthermore, he drew the conclusion from this case that the *Schutznormstheorie* was less exigent than the conditions which applied to article 173.

20. The expression *choices as to economic policy* is related to normative acts and serves the purpose to separate those acts from administrative acts which is important for incurring liability. This concept must probably be conceived to have a rather broad scope of application and include normative measures also concerning social policy, transport policy, freedom of establishment etc.

21. R.1975:549, consideration 44:
"qu'un l'absence d'un intéret public péremptoire, la Commission, en n'ayant pas assorti le règlement no 189/72 de mesures transitoires protégeant la confiance que l'opérateur pouvait légitimement avoir dans la réglementation communautaire, a violé une règle supérieure de droit et engagé ainsi la responsabilité de la Communauté".

22. See Goffin and Mahieu in *Cahiers 1972,* p. 87 f.

23. According to French and German administrative law the principle of *actori incumbit probatio* applies which however is modified by the investigation maxim, see further H Korsch in *Kölner Schriften zum Europarecht,* p. 130 f.

24. M Waline, *Précis de droit administratif,* p. 566.

Chapter seven

The damage

§ 7.1 The ECSC Treaty

Article 40 only states concerning the damage that a reparation in money shall take place, but there are no other indications as to the nature of the damage, and this has accordingly been left to the Court to decide upon. So far all cases dealing with damage have concerned economic losses; indemnity for physical injuries or damage on property has never been claimed.

The Court has expressed itself on the matter in the cases of *Worms* (R.VIII:401)

"un préjudice direct du fait d'une prétendue carence de la Haute Autorité...",

Feram (R.V:515)

"si cette majoration (of the tax of equalisation) entraine ou n'entraine pas,... et spécialement pour la requérante, un préjudice réel, appréciable et définitif...",

Meroni (R.VII:340)

"... l'application de l'article 40 suppose l'existence d'un préjudice actuel et certain...",

Feram (R.XI:414)

"que le préjudice invoqué par les requérantes n'est ni né ni actuel; qu'il s'agit tout au plus d'un préjudice futur, sans qu'il soit possible ni de l'éstimer immédiatement ni meme de considérer sa réalisation comme certain...",

Modena (R.X:449)

"...il n'est pas possible, à l'heure actuelle, de connaitre si et dans quelle mesure les requérantes subiront un préjudice à la suite de la liquidation des mécanismes financiers de la péréquation de la féraille et du décomte définitif des crédits et des dettes de chaque entreprise".

Accordingly the Court has attributed to the prejudice its characteristics of *direct, réel, né, certain, actuel, définitive, appréciable*. The word *direct* is evidently affiliated to the cause of link between the damage and the fact alleged to have brought about the damage, which is provided for in article 40 ("préjudice causé ... par une faute de service"). This question of causality is from a theoretical point of view not treated in an identical way in the laws of the

92

Member-States even if the results are often the same; it seems however that the Court in its deliberations has arrived at results close to the theory of *causalité adéquate* (see the cases of *Worms*, R.VII:383, *Laminoirs*, R.XI:1123 and *Temple*, R.IX:603). In the case where a Member-State is involved together with a community institution in causing damage, see the *Vloeberghs Case* (R.VII:475) and further § 7.2. For the time being it seems, considering that there are very few cases dealing with the damage itself, that a closer penetration of the question of causal connection would be unfruitful, other than establishing that there should be a very significant direct effect between the damaging fact and the prejudice; that is to say that one may follow the logical string that far so that the normal necessary effects of the damaging fact is covered and there one also looses the obvious connection—in fact a discretionary estimation in the concrete case. However, the Court has established a firm rule concerning the causal link when an institution has delivered misleading or incomplete information, which has led an individual to commit error. Here one notes the early case of *Temple* (R.IX:601) in which the Court examined the causal relationship between the fault and the alleged damage and stated that such an examination should include not only whether the behaviour of the institution concerned in fact had caused the error but also if it could and should have provoked such an error in the mind of a prudent person. This was not the case both in the above-mentioned affair and in the one of *Continentale* (R.1975:135f), and, besides, it was evident the plaintiffs themselves had been aware of the complete situation concerned; thus the causal link was interrupted, and the damage alleged was not caused by the contested behaviour of the institution.

The damage exists if it is *real*—not hypothetical—which means it is borne and certain; the criterion *borne* means that the facts constituting the damage are present; *certain* means that the realisation of the damage is a fact or its occurrence is considered to be certain in the future (*Heinemann Case*, R.XVIII:591f); accordingly the damage is actual. The word *definitive* might be interpreted as a limitation excluding later actions for supplementing claims for indemnity based on the same facts as within a first trial. However, this criteria seems not to be in conformity with rules in the laws of the Member-States. The damage must also be *evaluable* which means it is possible to estimate it in money.

In the only case (*Laminoirs*, R.XI:1124) but the civil servants' cases where the proceedings resulted in obliging the High Authority to pay indemnifications to the plaintiffs, the Court stated concerning the evaluation of the damage (p. 1158) that

"il est nécessaire de considérer une situation qui ne se serait produite si la faute n'avait pas été commise, le juge doit, tout en exigent le maximum de justifications, se contenter d'approximations sérieuses, telles que les moyens établies par comparaison".

In this case it was necessary to imagine the situation which should have occurred with regard to the iron bought for each factory concerned, if the promises of the transport subsidies relating to the specific period of time in question had not been given. The fact that it was difficult to estimate the damage was no reason for not judging the case even though it was a situation where certain elements could not be estimated exactly (R.XI:1165).

The evaluation of the damage involved many technical aspects which will not be mentioned here but the Court found those promises to provoke payments of indemnity to five applicants while nine were found not to have suffered any damage, since

"l'utilisation de ferailles navales, meme exonérées de la bonification de la parité de transport, a été moins onéreuse que celle de ferailles d'importation" (R.XII:203).

The damage was estimated as it occurred during the period of promises, and the indemnity paid does not take account of inflation or other currency changes.

Unlike article 34 there is no provision in article 40 stipulating a *special damage* which is a notion borrowed from the French system and does not exist in the German[1]. The Advocate-General Lagrange stated in the case of *Meroni* (R.VII:349) concerning the nature of a special damage[2]:

"l'illégalité a été commise à l'égard de toutes les entreprises sidérurgiques de la Communauté, . . . l'importance du préjudice varie selon les entreprises, mais, par sa nature, il n'est pas 'spécial' à l'une d'elles ou meme à une catégorie particulière."

Advocate-General Roemer stated in the *Vloeberghs Case* (R.VII:474):

"article 40 n'exige pas la preuve que la requérante seule ait subi un dommage . . . il suffit que la requérante, parmi un petit groupe bien déterminable, ait été la victime d'un événement dommageable".

One notes also Walter Much's[3] explanation of the effects of the special damage required in article 34:

". . .dass kein Kohle- oder Stahl-Unternehmen einen Schaden geltend machen kann, der z.B. durch eine allgemeine Entscheidung (Verordnung) der Hohen Berhörde allen Unternehmen der Gemeinschaft oder zumindest der überwiegenden Mehrzahl von ihnen in gleicher Weise zugefügt worden ist. . . Alle Unternehmen bilden in diesem Fall eine Verlustgemeinschaft".

Accordingly, in this article the coal and steel undertakings form the group to which *gene commun* does not provoke a claim for indemnity. In the case of *Meroni* (R.VII:334) the Court declared considering the existence of a damage:

"la Cour ne saurait reconnaitre que désavantages normaux, inhérents inévitablement au système de péréquation, constituent un préjudice donnant droit à réparation, et cela d'autant moins qu'ils frappent toutes les entreprises de la Communauté et que la péréquation apporte en contrepartie, à l'ensemble des utilisateurs de féraille, d'importants avantages. . . les requérantes n'ont pas établi l'existence d'un préjudice donnant droit à réparation"

and, besides, it added (p. 341) that it was not necessary in this case to ascertain whether article 40 presupposed a special damage or not and whether this condition was satisfied in that particular case[4]. In the *Simet Case* (R.XVII:214) the Court declared its earlier opinion on the whole but added:

"en l'espèce il n'a pas été établi que le désavantage subi par la requérante dépasserait celui normalement inhérent au système choisi ou ceux subis par ses concurrents;. . . attendu que ni l'existence d'une faute de service, ni celle d'un préjudice spécial de la requérante n'étant établies. . .".

In referring to article 34 as a *lex specialis* the Advocate-General Lagrange estamited in the case of *Meroni* (R.VII:351) that it was *not* appropriate to prescribe special damage in applying article 40, while the Advocate-General Roemer declared the opposite view in the case of *Vloeberghs* (R.VII:474) inasmuch as the provision for a special damage in article 34 was also applicable through analogous interpretation to article 40 when provoking a claim of responsibility in similar cases as under article 34 and called attention to the fact that in French administrative law the notion of *faute de service* implied in certain cases—but not in all—the necessity of a special damage. One notes in the *Laminoirs Case* (R.XII:200) where the Court granted indemnifications, that there was no discussion at all as to whether a special damage or not was required, but since not all undertakings of the Treaty or a major part of them were concerned the damage was special.

It is a fact that the equalisation system was adopted with its drawbacks as well as its advantages and that the decision to adopt the system evidently affected the political sphere; the disadvantages affected all the enterprises within the market—certainly not to the same extent—and raised the level under which no damage could be said to have been caused, and consequently, an enterprise must have suffered more than its competitors since otherwise there would not exist any damage. Note however, that according to French law the speciality and the gravity of the damage are inseparable (R Odent, *opus cited,* p. 1204).

The ECSC Treaty primarily affects the steel and coal undertakings which form a well defined group on which the financing of the Community mainly depends through the levy imposed on these enterprises. Third persons are thus only indirectly concerned but may of course suffer damage from the measures undertaken by the Community although the chance is obviously less in this case than for the steel and coal undertakings. It must be emphasised that the financial aspect is thus more salient in the context of this Treaty than in comparison with the Rome Treaties where the financial risk so to speak has been passed on to all persons of the Communities, moral as well as physical.

Therefore, the incorporation of a special damage in article 34 in order to avert unforseen claims and to limit the costs of running the Community is understandable. It would not be in conformity with the spirit of the Treaty to allow article 40 to give cause in certain cases to a financial end which is contrary to the aim of article 34. Therefore the suggestion forwarded by the Advocate-General Roemer appears to be perfectly wellfounded.

Concerning other persons than the coal and steel undertakings they will often be disqualified from obtaining indemnity due to the required infringement of a rule of law destined to protect their interests. Here also the action for indemnity cannot give rise to a financial end contrary to the aim of article 34.

Concerning the cases relating to the civil servants of the Community, they give no indications of the condition concerning the nature of a special damage. However, the condition will generally be satisfied. Furthermore, the general conditions described above concerning the nature of the damage are also true for the civil servants in their actions for indemnity unless the staff regulation in force at that time provides otherwise.

In article 40 it is provided that the Court is competent to order a pecuniary reparation from the Community[5] which speaks in favour of the reparation always being made in money, but it seems, however, not to be excluded (cf. the *Richez-Parise Case*) that the Court through a simple statement in a matter of procedure may be able to repair the damage, would abstain from doing so. Note, furthermore that the Court shall pursuant to article 34 (1) first sentence refer the matter back to the High Authority after the annulment, and in the case of the Community being liable, it shall use its powers according to the Treaty to ensure equitable redress for the harm suffered and shall only as a final resort pay appropriate damages; this seems not possible to do according to article 40 by analogous interpretation[6].

When there is both a *faute de service* and a fault on the part of the victim it is proper that the reparation be reduced; confer the statement of the Advocate-General Roemer in the *Vloeberghs Case* (p. 476):

"Il est évident que le préjudice aurait été moindre si elle (the plaintiff) avait agi ainsi".

Finally, it shall be mentioned that the Court accords reparation for moral damage,

"L'émotion causée par cette attitude, le trouble et le malaise qui en résultaient. . . ont dont causé aux requérants un dommage moral" (*Algera Case,* R.III:130)

at which the Court estimated the damage *ex aequo bona.*

§ 7.2 The Treaties of Rome

One notes from the case-law that here also the same qualities are attributed to the damage as in the ECSC Treaty; a real damage is required and not a hypothetical one (*Lasalle Case*, R.X:63), indemnity for moral damage is granted on which interest rate may not be counted (*Willame Case*, R.VI:804) and the damage must be *né et actuel* (*Richez-Parise Case*, R.XVI:339). In the *DiPillo Case*, (R.1973:772) the Court estimated the damage *ex aequo bona*.

In the cases of *Kampffmeyer* (R.XIII:318) and *Becker* (R.XIII:370) the Court distinguished between three categories of damage: a) plaintiffs who had carried out their concluded purchase-contracts and had paid the tax where the damage was due to the payment of the tax, since the plaintiffs had bought the maize on the expectation of no tax. The question was whether the damage would be repaired if the tax was reimboursed by the German authorities[7], and since the final answer to this question was not known, the Court considered the damage as not being *definitive*. The plaintiffs should also show that they only claimed damage for the contracts concluded on the 1st of October where they had relied upon the information of fixing the tax at zero in order to demonstrate the causal link; b) plaintiffs who also had acted according to the information delivered by the German authorities but cancelled their contracts, when refused importation licences, and to that end had paid indemnity, between which there was a *consequence directe;* they had thus a right to indemnity relating to the payments of cancellation but less what had been unnecessarily paid in excess thereof. The plaintiffs had also claimed indemnity for lost profits. This was partly dismissed by two arguments 1. the plaintiffs should have realised the abnormal situation and the possible mistake committed by the Commission in its decision of the 27th of September in fixing the price towards France; a fault on their own behalf seems to have been recognised[8] and 2. the commercial risk of the operations devolved upon the plaintiffs. The damage should be estimated *equitablement* to a sum not exceeding 10 % of what the plaintiffs should have paid in tax if the contracts had been executed; c) plaintiffs who had only demanded importation licences but not concluded any contracts and had lost expected profits. The Court considered these operations not to be concrete enough to give rise to indemnity; the damage was not certain.

These two cases show very well how closely linked together community and national measures can be i.e. the national authorities apply community legislation for a certain purpose which later on is endorsed by the Commission. However, the Commission's decision is declared illegal and annulled by the Court and the measures taken by the national authorities are also declared illegal by national courts, which raises the question of co-responsibility of the Community and the national authorities in both causing the damage occurred. Since the Court ordered the plaintiffs to exhaust national means both legal and administrative in order to obtain reimboursement of the unduly paid tax and present the judgements of their actions for indemnity against the German State before having the right to obtain any indemnity from the Community, this reveals the question whether the Community should merely be considered as subsidiarily responsible.

According to Achim André[9] a joint and severe responsibility exists not only in international law but also in the context of state liability in all the Member-States except France[10] in the meaning one may obtain execution against one of the parties being jointly responsible, who however has a right to recover what he has paid out in excess of his liability from the others. Furthermore, as to the primary or subsidiary responsibility of the Community there is nothing in the EEC Treaty itself which should support a subsidiary responsibility which also was the opinion sponsored by the Advocate-General in his submissions (R.XIII:361). Furthermore, one should also note that the authority *Einfuhr- und Vorratstelle für Getreide und Futtermittel* is a national organ designed to carry out the Community's agricultural policy[11].

If it is accepted that the Community and the German Republic are both primarily liable for damage they cause and that they can be held jointly responsible for the damage caused to the plaintiffs in the two above-mentioned cases, it remains only then to estimate the amount of the damage and distribute the indemnity to be paid in relation to the burden of guilt, but it is here that the problems arise, since the Court has only jurisdiction over the Community's liability and the German courts only over the German Republic's liability according to their distinct and different legal systems, although both authorities—the Commission and the German authorities—sometimes apply community law. The Court however cannot censure the national application of community rules, although it may by means of preliminary rulings directly assist national courts in interpreting community law but the application remains with the national authorities on the national level. This situation of two jurisdictions may result in different appreciations of the occurred damage and the amount of indemnity to be paid as well as the amount to be paid by each tortfeasor, which also concerns the questions of recovery actions and enforcement of judgements.

The issue of *Amtshaftungs-Konkurrenz zwischen EWG und Bundesrepublik Deutschland*[12], in which the plaintiffs had to fight a two-front battle complicated by the provision in BGB article 839 (1), second sentence, concerning the *Amtshaftung*[13], got partly a solution by the judgement of the *Bundesgerichtshof* (December 12, 1974, referred in NJW 1975, p. 491) from which one may understand that all maize importers from the affair of October 1, 1963 are entitled to obtain compensation from the German Republic (see comments by Elster, *opus cit.* page 254f). However, there remain many questions to be answered before the situation as to liability for a joint administration

98

by community and national organs can be considered to be clear, e.g. may a Member-State recover indemnity paid from the Community concerned[14].

It appears from article 215 (2) of the EEC Treaty that the Community shall have *caused* a damage, which expresses the causal link between the Community's action and the damage. It seems that until now, the Court has had the same view on this matter as in the ECSC Treaty. However, as it has been discussed above, the Community's influence on national legislation is a very complex matter which also affects the causal connection, and the *Lütticke Case* shows it may sometimes be very difficult for the plaintiff to demonstrate such a connection. In that case the Advocate-General Dutheillet de Lamothe considered the situation where the Commission had addressed a directive to the German Republic (R.XVII:347f) and found that the multifarious hypothetical situations which could appear after such a decision were quite sufficient to demonstrate the non-existence of a direct link of cause between the alleged damage and the behaviour of which the Commission was accused[15]. Note also the *Schöppenstedt Case* (R.XVII:1002), where the Advocate-General had difficulties in seeing the causal connection. However, in principle, such a connection may exist, and the Advocate-General Roemer pronounced in the case of *Vloeberghs* (page 475):

"Le fait que l'attitude contraire au traité d'un État membre est à l'origine d'un lien de cause à effet n'exclut pas que l'omission consécutive de la Haute Autorité soit considérée comme la cause directe du préjudice. Si la Haute Autorité a omis de faire usage de ses fonctions de controle à l'égard d'un État membre, elle est responsable du préjudice qui résulte du comportement primaire et contraire au traité d'un État membre".

This thesis was resumed by the Advocate-General Gand in the *Kampffmeyer Case* (page 360). In that case the Court, however, dismissed the Commission's argument that it was a controlling organ and only assumed responsibility in cases of *faute lourde,* since the Commission should here be as careful as the national authorities and assumed an independent liability for its maintenance of the safeguarding measure.

The question of a special damage as a requisite in article 215 (2) has so far not been discussed by the Court; however, the damage seems to have been special in the cases of *Kampffmeyer* and *Becker*. There seems to be no support in general either in the Treaty or in the laws of the Member-States regarding the case for a special damage.

According to the Treaties of Rome an institution whose act has been declared void must take the necessary steps to comply with the judgement of the Court, but this obligation (art. 176 (2) of the EEC Treaty) does not affect the outcome of the application of article 215 (2). In some cases these measures certainly will, if not enough to make good the damage, so at least be sufficient to reduce it; moreover, the Court may refer the matter back to the institution concerned for re-examination (cf. article 34 of the ECSC Treaty) which was done in the case of *Willame* (R.XI:829). It seems that the Court, according to the Treaties of Rome has a greater possibility by virtue of article 215 (2) to act than of article 40 of the ECSC Treaty, but certainly not to the extent of infringing upon the administrative and legislative competence of the Commission or the Council, since the former Treaty only says *make good damage,* where the latter speaks of a pecuniary reparation.

Concerning the methods of calculating the damage the *abstract* and *concrete* methods were brought into discussion in the cases of *Werhahn, Holtz & Willemsen, Continentale* and *CNTA.* The latter method was evidently followed in the procedure in the *Laminoirs Case,* since the Court considered the situation of each plaintiff in which no erroneuos promises had been given which resulted in a complete different outcome compared to the simple operation of calculating the amount of compensation which had been refused. The Advocate-General Roemer rejected in the *Werhahn Case* (p. 1272) a simple method similar to the one employed by the plaintiffs in the *Laminoirs Case* (abstract), since it was unknown to international law and could therefore not be embodied by article 215 (2) as a common principle to the laws of the Member-States. One should instead imagine the plaintiffs' situations without the element of discrimination which was the effect of the contested measures. When doing so, the calculation of the damage was a complex operation which suggested that an expert should be designated in order to clarify facts.

In the *Holtz & Willemsen Case* the Advocate-General Reischl (p. 708) thought that perhaps the plaintiff, in basing himself on the principle of equality of treatment, instead of claiming indemnity aimed at obtaining a subsidy similar to the one granted to factories in Italy, when insisting upon the applicability of the abstract method of calculating.

The same approach was adopted by the Advocate-General Trabucchi in the *Continentale Case* who declared that the damage did not necessarily coincide with the fraction of the subsidy demanded but not obtained. One had to take account of the economic result caused by the influence of the erroneous conviction on the contracts and their clauses. Since the exact amount of damage could not be established in this case, the Advocate-General referred to a principle generally applied in the Member-States in such a case, namely equity, i.e. a discretionary estimation based on all the circumstances of the case. In the *CNTA Case* (page 549) the Court pronounced that the damage to be repaired was not identical to the sums of subsidies concerned and added in consideration 46:

"que la protection à laquelle il peut prétendre en raison de sa confiance légitime n'est que celle de ne pas subir de pertes du fait de l'abrogation de ces montants".

The parties were invited to submit to the Court within a period of six months following the judgement the figure of the indemnity arrived at together. At default of such an agreement the parties should within the same delay submit their figures at which they had arrived.

Footnotes chapter seven

1. W Much, *Die Amtshaftung im Recht der Europäischen Gemeinschaft für Kohle und Stahl*, p. 50.

2. Note the French definition, R Odent, *Contentieux administratif*, IV, p. 1204:
"Le dommage spécial ou anormal est celui qui exède par son importance celui que supportent la générosité des intéressés",

which is required in the context of liability based on the theory of risk, see Chapter eight.

3. W Much, *opus cited above*, p. 50.

4. See R Odent, *opus cited*, p. 1197. When the liability is based on *faute de service* it is not necessary to look for a special or general damage.

5. R Odent, *opus cited*, p. 1196:
"Les dommages causés par des activités administratives ne peuvent donner lieu qu'à une réparation pecuniaire".

6. Cf. the statement made by the Advocate-General Lagrange in the case of *Chasse* (R.VIII:761) where he recommended the Court to refer the affair to the High Authority
"pour fixation et liquidation de l'indemnité due"

which is a method practiced in the French system, J Rivero, *opus cited*, p. 257.

7. The safeguarding measure had also been declared illegal at the national level.

8. See L Goffin in *Cahiers 1968*, p. 90 f and Advocate-General Roemer in the *Vloeberghs Case* (R.VII:476).

9. *NJW 1968*, pp. 331—336.

10. One notes from the French system that *Conseil d'État* when the state is held liable in *solidum* with a third person in certain cases has estimated the part of responsibility resting upon the state and has made a reduction of the indemnity to be paid by the state. In such a case there does not take place a recovery action before a civil court. Waline, *Précis de Droit Administratif*, p. 590.

11. See L Goffin's critical views in *Cahiers 1968*, p. 92 f.

12. H P Ipsen in *Europarecht 1969*, pp. 57—59. See further Theodor Elster in *CMLReview 1975*, pp. 90—100 and pp. 254—257, for an exhaustive description of the various tours before the Court and the national courts of Germany, which lasted for more than ten years.

13. This sentence reads:
"Fällt dem Beamten nur Fahrlässigkeit zur Last, so kann er nur dann in Anspruch genommen werden, wenn der Verletzte nicht auf andere Weise Ersatz zu erlangen vermag".

14. H Schermers, *opus cited*, p. 134, has the view that one may separate between acts of the Member-States committed in their capacity of *community organs* and *sovereign*

states. In the former case they act as agents of the Community, and one may then formulate a rule similar to that of the civil servants of the Communities, that the Communities shall make good any damage caused by their Member-States in the performance of their duties as Members. However, he remarks, there is no redress established for the indemnity paid by the Communities against the Member-States but thinks such rules could be derived from general principles of law common to the laws of the Member-States, although it has not yet been tried.

15. This was criticised by L Goffin in *Cahiers 1972,* p. 91.

Chapter eight

Liability without fault

§ 8.1 Survey of national systems of the Member-States with regard to liability without fault

8.1.1 France[1]

The general basis of liability without fault is the *rupture of equality* with respect to public charges imposed on the citizens. If a public authority undertakes measures in *the public interest* knowing in advance that these measures will or may injure certain persons in society inasmuch as a supplementary sacrifice is imposed on these persons affected by the measures, the rupture has to be corrected by an indemnity. *The theory of risk* i.e., someone is exercising a dangerous activity in relation to third persons and if the risk of damage occurs, indemnity has to be paid, covers and explains only a part of the field in which public authorities are held liable for damage caused but rupture of equality seems then to be the general formula[2].

There are legal provisions in statutes laying down rules of liability without fault on certain terms in the following cases: professional risks, damage resulting from riotous assemblage on the basis of *risque social,* national misfortune, accidents resulting from military preparation, accidents after obligatory inoculations, damage resulting from nuclear accidents based on ratified international conventions from Paris 1960 and 1964 and Brussels 1963 and supplemented by national provisions.

In the case-law several rules have been elaborated[3] for the incurring of liability;

a) dangerous activities or activities causing serious damage, e.g. the idea of an abnormal risk in relation of neighbourhood or the use by the police of exceptionally dangerous weapons or machines;

b) occasional co-operators in a public service suffering damage from that, conditioned by the co-operators havn't committed any fault themselves;

c) liability resulting from *les lois,* comprising all acts having legal force including ratified international conventions and treaties;

1) liability resulting from the legislative function: the state cannot be held liable because of the promulgation of a law as such and the legislator cannot thus be censured by courts in respect of a committed fault since it would infringe the sovereignty of the legislative function and the deliberate distri-

bution of power in society. However, it is nevertheless a fact that a law may be to the detriment of certain persons in society, and when taking a position on the matter of whether such a person is entitled to reparation one may distinguish between three cases: a) the law concerned explicitly accords indemnity b) refuses any right to indemnity c) the law is silent in that respect. In the last case it is necessary by means of interpretation to find out the probable intention of the legislator, hereby important elements are the objectives of the law, the preparatory works and circumstances of the case in their political, social and judicial context. The law must have been taken in the public interest but one presumes generally that the legislator never had the intention of granting indemnity to make good a damage resulting from a legislation ending up a moral, economic or social situation which is injurious to the public interest or an abuse of a certain situation even though there may be a rupture of equality, e.g. a law was introduced in 1915 prohibiting the production of absint. The producers, in their action for indemnity, claimed that this law had caused them damage; the action was dismissed on the grounds that the product concerned was injurious to the public health. A legislation issued solely in the general interest of the whole population will not incur state liability.

A further condition is that the nature of the damage must be *special* and of a *sufficient gravity* which is always required in actions for indemnity not based on a committed fault.

2) liability resulting from legal administrative decisions, of which one can distinguish between issued regulations, e.g. implementing the application of a law, and other decisions or measures by the administration; in both these cases the court has the possibility of declaring the measure to be illegal and entailing a fault capable of incurring the liability. Legal regulations — with the exclusion of measures taken in the interest of public order or in the general interest concerning economic matters — may incur liability on the same terms as those prevailing for laws. Concerning individual decisions and measures, they must also be taken in the public interest and sometimes the damage must also be exceptional besides being special in nature; there will be no reparation where the administration was not required to act, and the attitude of the victim must not have provoked the damaging measure. It is very rare that legal individual decisions give right to reparation, but one notes however, that refusal of execution of court decisions, by which the refusal may constitute a fault, can also be legal and motivated by higher considerations concerning the *paix publique* and give a right to reparation.

3) Finally, non-faulty administrative measures justified by the public interest can incur liability on the same terms as in 2) above.

8.1.2 Belgium[4]

In administrative law public authorities may be held liable without fault based on the principle of equality of public charges of the citizens giving compensation for exceptional damage suffered resulting from the functioning of a service. *Conseil d'État* considers, from the viewpoint of equality, the exceptional character of the damage and other circumstances in the particular case without any attention being paid to a fault on the part of the administration concerned. However, the competence of the *Conseil d'État* is merely subsidiary, since it can only express its view on the matter and is unable to deliver a binding judgement on the administration which is incumbent on the civil courts. Concerning legal acts the civil courts seem to be unable to award indemnity for damage resulting from such acts. The liability is mainly developed in the field of public works.

8.1.3 Luxembourg[5]

The theory of equality of public charges is not applicable in general but with the exception of damage caused by public works. The Supreme Court decided by judgement in 1937 that the state is not allowed to make good damage resulting from laws.

8.1.4 Italy[6]

The state liability derives from an intentional or faulty action by a civil servant in his performance of duties on behalf of the state. The anonymous fault by a service (*faute de service*) is not developed. The fault is mostly presumed from the existence of an illegal or illicit fact. The action must also have infringed a subjective right of the injured person but one can also see a tendency towards extending the liability to repair damage occured when a legitimate interest has been violated. There are certain cases of strict liability corresponding to the ones in civil law (*Code Civil*, artt. 2045 *et subs.*) mainly based on the risk of occurrence of damage.

A law being unconstitutional is considered to be unable by itself to incur liability, since a parliamentary action does not constitute an illegal behaviour giving rise to a damaging fact, but the law may, when being applied cause damage which can be made good on the terms mentioned above. There seems to be no liability for legal acts.

8.1.5 Holland[7]

The state liability is mainly based on article 1401 in *Burgerlijk Wetboek* which reads:

"Jedes unrechtmässige Verhalten, das einem anderen Schaden zufügt, verpflichtet denjenigen, dessen Schuld den Schaden verursacht hat, zur Entschädigung".

Liability is only incurred if the unlawful action is attached to guilt (*Schuld*) committed by the state organs or officials of the state. The injured person need not look for a guilty person in an administration but may sue the administration concerned itself before a civil court, which will then generally presume the guilt if someone has acted unlawfully; the official who carried out the measure may be innocent though the administration may be liable. The state is not liable for damage resulting from unconstitutional laws, regulations etc when the formal procedure of issuing the act has been followed; but implementing administrative regulations may be illegal and incur liability in connection with a burden of guilt. By the development of the jurisprudence the state has also been held liable for dangerous activities based on risk; there is also said to be a tendency for liability of legal acts or measures.

8.1.6 Germany[8]

In the German system of public liability one speaks of three different types of indemnifications:

a) *Schadenersatzleistung* results from public liability and is the indemnity caused by a civil servant's faulty (*Verschulden*) and illegal acting (art. 34 GG and art. 839 BGB); articles 840—853 of BGB give further rules on the matter including *inter alia* provisions concerning the damage and the indemnity. The possibilities for obtaining indemnity suffer from certain limitations even though the state liability in itself has been enlarged by interpretation.

b) *Entschädigung* is the indemnity resulting from state liability provoked by state intervention based on and developed from the concept of expropriation. Here it concerns basically the guarantee for and the use of property owned by private persons for which rules have been established in article 14 GG, which reads:

1. Das Eigentum und das Erbrecht werden gewährleistet. Inhalt und Schranken werden durch die Gesetze bestimmt.

2. Eigentum verpflichtet. Sein gebrauch soll zugleich dem Wohl der Allgemeinheit dienen.

3. Eine Enteignung ist nur zum Wohle der Allgemeinheit zulässig. Sie darf nur duch Gesetz oder auf Grund eines Gesetzes erfolgen, das Art und Ausmass der Entschädigung regelt. Die Entschädigung ist unter gerechter Abwägung der Intressen der Allgemeinheit und der Beteiligten zu bestimmen. Wegen der Höhe der Entschädigung stellt im Streitfalle der Rechtsweg vor den ordentlichen Gerichten offen.

The expropriation (*Enteignung*) as means of supply of property has not caused any particular problems in applying this article, but the word has also got a broader conception in separating those situations which do and which do not give rise to compensation where the difference between *Enteignung und Eigentumsbeschränkung* depends on the gravity of the lawful intervention. As a negative rule one may say that compensation is normally excluded

"wer bei der Verwaltung gegenüber bestehenden Pflicht gefasst wird".

In the early nineteen fifties the field of compensation was extended by jurisprudence to *enteignungsgleiche Eingriff* which is characterised by an illegal intervention by the state in the sphere of the law of individuals having from a legal viewpoint, regarding its content as well as the effect produced, the nature of an expropriation and by that creating a particular sacrifice to the person concerned. Under this concept a civil court may grant compensation when the intervention is based on a rule of law not in force, and on an application impaired by legal vice of a rule of law in force, or on a rule not in force, which is *inter alia* applicable to *Verfassungswidrige Legislative Akte*.

Compensation has also been granted for damage caused by faulty illegal expropriaton or expropriationlike interventions which overlaps the *Amtshaftung* in article 839 BGB.

To these rules one should also add the institute of *Aufopferanspruch* covering *hoheitlichen Eingriff* giving compensation for physical injuries caused. One could probably also refer to this remedy when the system of expropriationlike intervention fails provided there is a *hoheitlichen Eingriff* in the rights of an individual or his protected interests which has been conducted in the public interest causing a damage and having the nature of a particular sacrifice to the individual.

c) *Entschädigung* is also indemnity resulting from state liability on the terms of risk provided for in special legislation and further developed by the courts. The notion has a more narrow scope of application than the one in the French system.

8.1.7 United Kingdom[9]

The old English system did not respond to the increased scope of state interference which forced the courts by means of legal fictions to alleviate situations of obvious injustice. Not until 1947 was the *Crown Proceedings Act* adopted making the Crown at least subject to the same liability in torts as private citizens of full age and capacity implying that the master and servant are jointly responsible and severely when the servant has committed a tort but also imposing a non-vicarious liability based on the direct duty of the master. Though the Crown is subject to private law by the Act, it is done so with serious reservations limiting the scope of liability, and it is furthermore important to distinguish between organs of the Crown and other public bodies of which the former is ruled by the Act and the latter mainly by private law as private citizens. Most tortious liability requires intentional or negligent action.

The Crown will be subject to liability without fault in such cases where private citizens are held liable which is a rather restricted field concerning for example dangerous things[10]. There is no state liability incurred for the activities of its parliamentary assemblies nor from the laws unless a law itself accords indemnity.

8.1.8 Ireland and Denmark[11]

The Irish system follows mainly the English.

The Danish state is liable for dangerous operation by the police causing damage but probably also under extraordinary circumstances for e.g. concrete legal acts.

§ 8.2 The ECSC Treaty

As follows from the foregoing survey of the national systems of state liability in the Member-States, one can see a general tendency in all countries — of which France evidently has the most developed system — in direction towards a more extensive state liability though only a few of them have reached beyond the traditional areas of liability; accordingly the extent of the common basis of principles in this area of state liability may be disputed. The tendency to make the state liable to a continuously larger extent is however conceivable, since the various state activities are increasingly intervening and regulating the private lives of citizens, which sometimes puts the judge in a precarious situation, since the general legal framework impedes him from coping with the changing situation and doing justice.

The question is, however, whether the ECSC Treaty might accord community liability beyond the system of *faute de service* and *faute personelle*; this seems, however, rather unlikely, since the Treaty itself provides explicitly in article 34 and as well as in article 40 (1) and (2) the necessary requisite for a fault. This would accordingly speak in favour of excluding the Community from repairing damage resulting from illegal actions devoid of any attachment to fault and accordingly also legal actions, since a legal action can never be faulty by its nature.

In two early cases from the Court the item of liability beyond *faute de service* was touched upon (*Feram Case*, R.V:516 and *Chasse Case*, R.VIII:725) in so far as the plaintiffs invoked a passage in the considerations in one of the decisions establishing the equalisation system (decision 14/55) where the High Authority had declared itself responsible for the regular functioning of the system. However, the Court pronounced that such a statement did not constitute a commitment to the enterprises, subjects to the compulsory system, or a guarantee creating a contractual liability, or any legal or objective responsibility incumbent on the High Authority also in the event of no fault being attributable. It seems then that a liability without a *faute de service* is excluded as a principle[12], but the actual scope of liability may in practice be extended, if desired, in the sense that the Court is more easly convinced of the existence of a fault.

However, one notes from article 40 (3) that all other disputes between the Community and persons other than its servants (not only encompassing indemnity actions) outside the application of the articles of the Treaty and implementing legislation relating to it shall take place before national jurisdiction. The issue remains then to determine what is outside or inside the application of the articles of the Treaty but theoretically this evidently means that the Community can be held liable within the scope of non-contractual liability before national jurisdictions according to national legislation without having committed a fault[13].

§ 8.3 The EEC Treaty

One notes here immediately that the situation is completely different compared to the ECSC Treaty, since the institutions pursuant to article 215 (2) shall make good the damage caused by them in accordance with general principles common to the laws of the Member-States which will thus determine the scope of liability. A closer penetration of the interpretation and meaning of this passage relating to the principles shall however not be anticipated here but be subjected to examination in the next chapter entitled Applicable law; the description shall therefore be limited to the development of the case-law as such on this matter.

In the *Kampffmeyer Case* (R.XIII:322) the concept of liability without fault was touched upon in the arguments put forward by the plaintiffs, but the Court did not respond to these hints[14]. The item was resumed in the case of *Schöppenstedt* (R.XVII:975) as a subsidiary claim for compensation which was not based on a fault but on the detriment caused by the regulation concerned. However, the claim lacked precision and was accordingly considered as being inadmissible by the Court.

The pleading of "la rupture de l'égalité des citoyens devant les charges publiques" was explicitly made for the first time in the *CIE Case* (R.XVIII:

395) where the damage caused was alleged to be abnormal and special. The Court took a cautious view through writing "a possible responsibility resulting from a legal normative act" but obviously made its considerations from the viewpoint of the arguments put forward by the plaintiffs and since it found the action not well-founded, this must imply a recognition of the remedy as such[15]. However, the circumstances in the particular case were not susceptible of incurring liability, since the measures undertaken by the Commission quite obviously had the nature of securing the public order with regard to economic matters which corresponds perfectly well to the rules elaborated within the French system. Furthermore, the criteria for a special and abnormal damage were not satisfied[16].

The plaintiffs had in the *Werhahn Case* (R.1973:1229) invoked the German concept of expropriationlike illegal intervention as a remedy for obtaining compensation of alleged damage suffered in an action subsidiary to the one based on fault. The Court remarked that, since the criticised acts had not been found illegal, it was not necessary to develop the question of whether article 215 (2) accorded responsibility on such terms.

Furthermore, one notes incidently that the considerations by the Court on the two remedies invoked in the *CIE Case* were headed
"1. Sur le moyen tiré de l'illegalité . . ."
and
"2. Sur le moyen tiré de la responsabilité en absence d'illegalité . . ."
while in the *Werhahn Case* the subsidiary claim with its arguments was not considered as a separate remedy in the layout of the judgement but treated in the same section and context as the principal action based on the faulty illegality of the acts concerned. However, one should not exaggerate these formal viewpoints bearing in mind that it was from a material view completely unnecessary to take a position on the matter in order to adjudicate the *Werhahn Case* and thus also to consider the remedy as such. Considerations in that respect would necessarily have compelled the Court to decide explicitly upon the matter of liability without fault which would primarily implied an interpretation of the law applicable in the context of article 215 (2) and secondly, if necessary, the creation of rules of law in harmony with the already adopted system provided no change in that system was intended. Without profoundly trying to estimate the value of the French *rupture* and the German *expropriationlike intervention* within their national systems respectively, the general remark shall only be made here that both concepts purport to compensate for detriment suffered in exceptional situations by state interference, where the *rupture* has the advantages compared with the German notion in clearly showing its own purpose, having a broader field of application, being more flexible and will of course easily fitting into the *faute de service* system.

§ 8.4 The EAEC Treaty

8.4.1 General

The Euratom Treaty must be seen in its context of supply-shortage of fuels resulting from the Suez crisis in 1956 and the prevailing optimistic beliefs at that time in a fast an practical application of nuclear energy for the needs of society. With the different directions of development of the European coal and steel industries in mind, it was an obvious advantage to establish a European basis for the development and use of nuclear energy at least in its civil application — even though the Treaty itself does not impede the Community from building nuclear bombs or forbid military applications on a national level. However, the expectations of the authors of the Treaty have not come true, since the importance of nuclear energy only plays a minor role compared with other sources of supply of energy, depending on among many things difficulties of integration in the field of commercial application.

The objectives of the Treaty are to be found in articles 1 and 2 from which one notes *inter alia* the promotion of research which has been so far the main activity carried out in various research-centres administered by the Commission, and in common projects with Member-States, but the Community has also participated in projects with third countries. Research is also promoted by means of joint undertakings (artt. 49—51). Furthermore, the Community shall

"secure that all users in the Community receive a regular and equitable supply of ores and nuclear fules"

for that purpose a *Supply Agency* (see § 4.4.2) was envisaged in article 52: 2 (b). The Agency has a right of option on nuclear material produced within the Member-States and an exclusive right to conclude contracts relating to such materials regardless of whether the materials originate from the Community or third countries. The Agency did not play an important role during the sixties but is now achieving a growing importance depending on the enlargement of the Community, the indications of changing market conditions of nuclear materials from buyers' to the sellers' market and also in the prospect of increased importance of nuclear energy resulting from the energy crisis of autumn 1973. The Commission stresses[17] the importance of laying down a Community energy policy in which the nuclear energy will be a dominant element. Therefore there are reasons to believe there will be a vitalisation of the Euratom with increased activities and a higher degree of cooperation. The interest in this chapter will be focused on the community liability resulting from nuclear operations, since operations causing damage other than nuclear will certainly follow the developments under the EEC Treaty.

However, one should observe some special provisions in the context of dissemination of information and more specifically related to the compulsory communication of certain applications for patents or utility models relating to nuclear matters to the Commission which are filed in a Member-State. When such unpublished applications are improperly used or brought to the knowledge of unauthorised persons, the Community shall make good damage suffered by the party concerned (art. 28). This evidently concerns the non-contractual liability of the Community; although no references are made to a fault nor to the general provision in article 188 (2), but it is plainly stated that the Community shall make good the damage suffered, one may perhaps presume the Court is competent. The Community assumes here the role of guarantor that the damage is actually repaired which appears from the second paragraph of article 28 laying down rules for actions for recovering of paid indemnity against the person responsible for the damage. Accordingly this is a special situation expressly bringing objective liability on the Community by the Treaty itself[18].

8.4.2 International conventions on liability for damage resulting from nuclear operations[19]

The international conference, held on the Peaceful Uses of Atomic Energy, in Geneva in September 1955 gathered about 1.400 representatives from 73 countries. In the conference information was disclosed on nuclear research which previously had been considered as secret or restricted data. This created the right atmosphere for establishing national as well as international bodies concerned with nuclear energy, such as the International Atomic Energy Agency (IAEA), European Nuclear Energy Agency (ENEA) and the Euratom (all occupied with peaceful purposes). The first international convention on Third Party Liability for Nuclear Damage was concluded in Paris 1960 under the auspices of the OECD. A supplementary Convention was concluded in Brussels in 1963 between almost the same nations. In 1963 The Vienna Convention on Civil Liability for Nuclear Damage was adopted on a wider basis under the IAEA sponsorship containing the same main principles as the Paris Convention. With the purpose to eliminate as far as possible any disparities between the Paris and Vienna Conventions the former was amended in a Protocol in 1964 and the Brussels convention was aligned to the amended one of Paris. The amended Paris Convention has been signed by all the Member-States with the exception of Ireland and ratified by Belgium, France and Great Britain. The same Member-States signing the Paris Convention have signed the Brussels Convention but only France and Great Britain have ratified it. That Convention has been ratified by five states in total and will come into force when the number of six ratifications are made which is likely to happen relatively soon through the accession of Denmark to both the Conventions. Though only a few of the Member-States have ratified the Conventions that doesn't mean they are devoid of national legislation in this respect but the principles of the Conventions have been the source of inspiration to the national legislators.

Concerning nuclear ships to which the above mentioned Conventions do not apply (only to land-based plants) one notes the International Convention for Safety of Life at Sea, dealing with safety standards, which is not applicable to war-ships contrary to the Convention on the Liability of Operators of Nuclear Ships adopted in Brussels 1962, which has not yet entered into force and probably never will. Bilateral agreements have instead been concluded between the state of the guest nuclear ship and the host state regulating questions of liability, radiation protection etc.

The general principle for liability in the Paris and Vienna Conventions for nuclear accidents is objective liability without any fault channeled to one single person, namely the operator of the nuclear plant. However, there are two exceptions of liability, when the accident is due to acts of armed conflict or civil war and to grave national disaster of exceptional character. Concerning the extent of the liability the operator is not subject to objective liability for the nuclear installation itself and property related to it, nor for damage to the means of transport for which special rules are provided. The amount of liability is fixed in the Vienna Convention at a minimum level of 5 million US dollars with no definite limit upwards for the liability of the operator counted per accident which is a limit to be decided by the national legislator. In the Paris Convention the amount of liability of the operator is fixed at a maximum level of 15 million of European Monetary Agreement units of account though allowing the contracting parties to establish a greater amount and with the minimum level at 5 million units of account. Article 15 of the Paris Convention allows a state to compensate damage from public funds on terms other than those provided for in the Convention in excess of the minimum level. The Brussels Convention is concerned with state intervention for compensating damage caused by an accident up to the amount of 120 million units of account. This state compensation is comprised in a three-stage-system:
1) national provisions for the operator's liability (5—15 million units of account);
2) compensation out of public funds by the state in whose territory the plant is situated up to the amount of 70 million units of account counted from the ceiling in 1), and,
3) the range between 70 and 120 million units of account is covered by public funds from the contracting parties as a whole.

One of the conditions for applicability of the Convention is that damage and liability under the Paris Convention are concerned. The liability is limited in time to ten years from the date of the accident unless the accident is due to stolen, lost, jettisoned or abandoned materials then there will be a period of limitation of twenty years from the theft etc.

Concerning transport, the liability has been put on the operator who is liable up to the point when another operator assumes liability under express terms in a contract or when taking charge of the materials. Special rules are incorporated when the nuclear material comes from a non-contracting state.

Competent courts according to the Paris Convention are those of the contracting party within whose territory the accident occurred — which is the system also incorporated in the Brussels Convention. Such judgements are enforceable in the other contracting states without a re-examination of their content. To cover his liability the operator has to have and maintain an insurance or other financial security. The construction of the insurance policies to meet the prescribed obligations of the operator is a topic which shall not be examined here, since it falls outside the subject to be dealt with.

8.4.3 Community liability

Article 188 (2) of the Treaty prescribes as well as article 215 (2) of the EEC Treaty that the Community shall make good damage caused by its institutions, of which the Commission is the institution administering the nuclear operations, in accordance with principles common to the laws of the Member-States; the Court is exclusively competent in such disputes pursuant to article 151 compared with article 155. Notwithstanding any interpretation of those principles claiming for applicability it must be considered as certain that the Community assumes objective liability for nuclear accidents towards third parties in acting in the capacity of an operator which is a rule commonly recognised by the laws of the Member-States. However, one can not consider this field of law as unified — disregarding the fact that only a few of them have ratified the Conventions — since the Paris and Brussels Conventions themselves leave many items unregulated for the benefit of the national legislator such as procedural rules, proof of damage, modalities for recovery of the damage, the financial guarantees of the operator's liability. The national legislations based on the Conventions seem then to appear as more a special branch of and incorporated into the national context of non-contractual liability and also brought into harmony with social security legislation and other relevant national legislation. Furthermore, one should note that the Community has issued several directives on health and safety standards which thus are forming a common basis (artt. 30—39 of the Treaty). However, one may expect that the Court will in deciding the law applicable turn primarily to the Conventions as such as being the real basis of origin of the common principles behind the laws of the Member-States, secondly, supplement them where appropriate with existing community law and thirdly look to solutions adopted by national legislation. Fortunately, indeed, there hasn't been any accident and nor is there any case-law, and hopefully there will not be any; however, from a theoretical viewpoint the position regarding community liability will presumably manifest itself as follows.

The Community's operations and activities in the nuclear field take place in different forms. Firstly, the Commission is running and administering the Community's own research-centres in Ispra (Italy), Mol (Belgium), Karlsruhe (Germany) and Pettern (Holland) and thus acting in the capacity of operator of these plants. Financial safeguards have been taken by the Commission to meet liability for damage resulting from nuclear accidents towards third persons in terms of insurances concluded with the national insurance companies in the countries where the plants are situated, but for the plant in Karlsruhe public guarantees have been given to cover damage.

In view of the discrepancies between the national legislations indicated above it seems urgent to touch upon some specific questions.

Sometimes the national legislation admits (e.g. the Swedish) the injured person to seek indemnity directly from the insurer. In such a case where the Community's liability is concerned the national courts will be incompetent to judge the dispute, since that question belongs exclusively to the Court to judge upon, and the insurer is only by a contractual obligation towards the Community forced to meet the liability incumbent on the Community to the extent that the contractual agreements admit. Where there is disaccord between the Community and the insurer this contractual dispute has to be settled, if necessary e.g. before a court, which might very well be the Court in force of a prorogation clause pursuant to article 153 of the Treaty, but until now the actual contracts concluded contain a prorogation clause to national courts in the country where the plant is situated and supplemented with a choice-of-law clause in favour of the national law concerned. However, most indemnifications to victims will probably in fact be settled outside any court proceedings in negotiations between the Commission, the victims and the insurer.

However, there are many delicate detailed questions which may arise before the Court but attempts shall not be made here to solve them but merely to indicate some of them, since due to their complex nature the uncertainty in forecasting solutions is considerable and such suggestions are accordingly of a minor interest.

In article 6 of the Paris Convention reference is made to national legislation concerning the right to benefit from the relevant social security system and the right of recovery for such authorities or institutions against the operator. It is easy to imagine a rather complex situation arising before the Court involving several national legislations. Furthermore pertinent questions will also be the importance of the nationality of the victims and the position of the employees of the operator. The period of limitation of a claim for indemnity is prescribed to be five years from the event causing the damage in the Statute of the Court, article 44, but the Paris Convention stipulates 10 years and 20 years under certain circumstances which is a conflict certainly not easy to conciliate. If the accident has been caused by serious negligence or intention, that behaviour may according to national legislation have consequences under penal law, but community law does not comprise criminal proceedings in that sense[20] but a possibility is that the institution concerned waives the immunity accorded to officials and other agents in order to enable prosecution under national law, which the Community shall do, if it is not contrary to the interest of the Community (art. 18 of the Protocol on the Previleges and Immunities of the EC).

The Community has also been involved in joint-undertakings under the auspices of ENEA such as Eurochemic, the Halden and Dragon projects[21]. These engagements, however, have not been susceptible to incur a direct Community liability due to their own legal constructions. Research contracts[22] have been concluded between the Community and various research institutions in which the community has not assumed the capacity of operator.

Finally, the Community can financially participate in *joint undertakings*[23] formed according to the rules in articles 45—51 of the Treaty. Such an enterprise is established by a unanimous Council decision on proposal by the Commission and is thereby endowed with a legal personality which may enjoy the most extensive legal capacity under the Member-States' laws and shall be governed by the Treaty, its own statutes, and rules applying to industrial or commercial undertakings, and its statutes may also make subsidiary references to the laws of the Member-States. When competence is not conferred upon the Court by the Treaty national courts or tribunals have competency.

The diversity of references to applicable law to govern such entities has probably been made with respect to the presumed participants (see art. 46, mom. 1, sections d) and e)) involving a possible ownership of not only the Member-States and subjects to their national laws but also third states[24], international organisations or nationals of third states, of whom not all are subjected to domestic law where in such a case community law will provide a suitable legal personality in the event where no other legal system does. However, the joint undertakings are in practice entities which appear as national legal entities as GmbH, S.A. etc. where the Council decision establishing the status of a joint undertaking (endowed primarily with tax privileges) is incorporated into the statutes of the company as well as other relevant provisions of the Treaty and the statutes of the company is annexed to the Council decision[25]. Accordingly the undertaking enjoys legal capacity under both national as well as community law, of which the latter ensures recognition in all Member-States. The Court is competent (art. 49 (5)) to make rulings on the Council decision, provisions of the Treaty and other community rules related and applicable to the company when competency has been conferred by the Treaty while the company with regard to other matters remains subject to the national law under which it was created and also to the rules of liability for nuclear accidents provided for in that law. Accordingly, even though the Community may participate as a financier in such a project, it will not be liable itself, but only the company according to the terms of the national law[26].

However, one can conceive a situation in which states and private companies enter into a consortiumlike agreement for a certain purpose which is decided by the Council to constitute a joint-undertaking. In such a case the agreement to cooperate will merely enjoy legal personality by virtue of the Council decision according to community law. A victim of a nuclear accident can sue the undertaking before the national courts (art. 49 (3), last sentence), and since the undertaking can neither be construed as an institution nor in general as an agent of the Community, jurisdiction of the Court cannot accordingly have been conferred by the Treaty concerning non-contractuel liability (art. 49 (5)) and consequently only national courts are left for actions concerning liability for nuclear accidents as recourse. The question as to which courts will be competent one may expect that the courts in the country where the accident occurred will be competent and apply national legislation.

Concerning the position of the Supply Agency, it has the possibility of being the owner of fissionable materials and seems through that to be able to assume liability as operator, but in reality the liability is always passed on to an operator of a plant by contractual stipulations and the Agency accordingly escapes any liability (see further Part III).

Footnotes chapter eight

1. M Waline, *Précis de droit administratif*, pp. 567—586 and R Odent, *Contentieux administratif*, pp. 1122—1135.

2. Note F-P Bépoit, *Le droit administratif francais*, p. 712, who has the view that no general rule has been laid down or can be described, since the liability has been justified by various reasons.

3. M Waline, *Précis de droit administratif*, p. 580, makes the remark that there has been a tendency during recent years to make the state a kind of universal guarantor against all kinds of risks.

4. P Wigny, *Droit Administratif*, p. 300 f and C Cambier in *Haftung des Staates*, p. 54.

5. E Arendt in *Haftung des Staates*, p. 455 and T Biever in *Livre jubilaire du Conseil d'État, 1856—1956*, p. 457.

6. S Galeotti in *Haftung des Staates*, p. 300 f.

7. W F Prins in *Haftung des Staates*, p. 488 f.

8. E Forsthoff, *Lehrbuch des Verwaltungsrechts I*, pp. 290—339, and G Jaenicke in *Haftung des Staates*, p. 124 f. The whole law of non-contractual liability of public authorities is suggested to be replaced by new legislation, see H J Papier in *Deutsches Verwaltungsblatt 1974*, p. 573.

9. F A G Griffith and H. Street, *Principles of administrative law*, p. 255 f, H W R Wade, *Administrative law*, p. 277 f, and *Charles Worth on negligence* by R Perry, p. 240 f, and H Street in *Haftung des Staates*, pp. 230—248.

10. Note the remark by R Piret in a general report concerning the English report delivered by G H L Fridman who had enumerated a great number of cases giving liability without fault, that the majority of those cases pertained under continental conception to liability with fault. Centre interuniversitaire de droit comparé, *5th Congrès de droit comparé à Bruxelles*, p. 241 f.

11. P Germer in *Juristen 1967*, p. 460.

12. See L Goffin in *Droit des Communautés Européennes*, p. 144, where he rejects a liability without fault. Note the comments by Gérard Nafilyan in *Revue Trimestrielle de Droit Européen 1972*, p. 463 upon the case of *Feram* (R.XVII:227), in which he interprets *attendu* 27 and 28 as the Court reserves the question of liability without fault and leaves the matter open. However, it is not entirely certain whether the Court intended a responsibility beyond fault considering the statements in the context of the discussion of the nature of the damage *itself*. The Advocate-General Lagrange stated in the *Feram Case* (R.V:527):
"Pourquoi cette exigence (of a fault), qui exclut toute possibilité de faire appel à la théorie du risque? Sans doute, Messieurs, parce que les conditions de fonctionnement des institutions de la C.E.C.A. n'ont pas paru aux auteurs du traité de nature à créer ce risque anormal, qui seul pourrait justifier l'existence d'une responsabilité sans faute".

13. The same is applicable to the Rome Treaties, see articles 183 and 155 respectively.

14. Note also the statement by the Advocate-General Roemer in the case of *Plaumann*, R.IX:249, where he considered a liability without fault.

15. Note, however, that H Schermers, *opus cited*, p. 129, does not consider the case-law of the Court so far to recognise liability for lawful acts.

16. See the submissions by the Advocate-General Mayras, p. 425 f.

17. See e.g. *Bulletin of the EC*, Supplement 6/73, p. 8 and Energy for Europe, *SEC (74 2542 final*.

18. H Schermers, *opus cited*, p. 129, does not think one should from this provision by means of *a contraria* interpretation exclude an objective liability following from art. 188 (2).

19. See *Nuclear Law for a developing world*, IAEA, legal series nr 5, *Law relating to nuclear energy* by H Street and F R Frame, *Third colloque de droit européen*, Paris 1965, and La résponsabilité de l'Euratom, *Droit Nucléaire Européen*, Colloque 1966 in Paris.

20. Note in this context the draft conventions on criminal law relating to community officials, *The Eight General Report of the EC*, p. 76 f.

21. Of these at least Eurochemic must be characterised as a public international corporation, see GOZ Sundström, *The public international utility corporation*, p. 38 f.

22. For example the association contract with *Centre Belge d'Études d'Energie Nucléaire*.

23. See H-T Adam, *Les organismes internationaux spécialisés,* p. 79 f.

24. Cf. the international public utility corporation, see GOZ Sundström, *opus cited,* p. 106 f.

25. See Council decision 4/6/74 (O.J. L165/7) establishing the joint undertaking *Hoch-temperatur-Kernkraftwerk GmbH.*

26. See Adam, opus cited, p. 81.

Chapter nine

Applicable law

§ 9.1 The Court and its methods of interpretation[1]

To understand the Court's general approach towards the interpretation and application of the Treaties and supplementing community law, which is necessary in order to appreciate article 215 (2) and the reference expressed there to common principles of the laws of the Member-States, it seems necessary not only to point out the methods actually employed by the Court but also briefly to touch upon the position of the Court in the community legal framework[2] and that legal system's relation to domestic law as well as to international law.

The EEC Treaty is a document of programme-declarations to a much greater extent than the ECSC and EAEC Treaties, which seems to narrow the scope of action of the Court concerning the latter Treaties, but all three have nevertheless to be carried out in reality by means of implementation i.e. issuing rules detailed enough to be of practical guidance to persons affected by the Treaties. This is done by the legislating institutions (the Council and the Commission) who in their day-to-day work also interpret and apply the Treaties and implementing legislation issued earlier and accordingly in this way are developing and filling gaps in the legal framework. In this implementing process the Court plays an important role in guiding and correcting the direction according to its own concepts of the conformity with the Treaties and subsequent legislation of the measures undertaken by the other institutions, which thus implies an ultimate precision of the meaning of the Treaties themselves. Regarding the implementing measures of the Treaties the Court cannot replace such a one deemed to be illegal and perhaps abrogated with new positive rules of its own and in such a way create law, but that activity of the Court could instead be described as giving details and explanations of words and articles in the Treaties and subsequent legislation in a community sense, but also in another way. Since the community law is not comprehensive in comparison with a national legal system, the Court will find itself very often in the situation of having an issue raised for which community law provides no rules at all or merely gives an indication of direction for a solution, such as article 215, and is so vague in its nature that it cannot serve as such in achieving a solution to the concrete problem. The Court cannot however escape such a situation by declaring that the community law is devoid of rules relevant to the item in hand, since then, it would in a broad sense commit a *déni de justice* being evidently contrary to the Treaties (see e.g. art. 164 EEC), but has in some way to find a solution to the problem, i.e. the creation of positive rules of law.

The determination of the meaning of the Treaties and subsequent law is of course not unaffected by the arguments put forward by the other institutions, the Member-States, individuals[3], not to mention the Advocates-General. One could say that the Court in cooperation with the other institutions is eminently carrying out the Treaties. It is emphasised, however, that the Court has the final power to censor measures undertaken as to their legality but not appropriateness. In doing so, it obviously concerns the working methods of the Court of which not all can be disclosed by studying various community texts themselves but only by the case-law as such.

One notes from the early case-law of the Court in dealing with the ECSC Treaty *inter alia* the case of the *French Republic versus the High Authority* (R.I:23) in which the Court clearly exposed some of its ways of reasoning as well as how it regarded it own position. Concerned with the interpretation of article 60 of the Treaty it started its argument by the following:

"Les articles 2, 3 et 4 du Traité, mentionnés en tete du paragraphe 1 de l'article 60, constituent des dispositions fondamentales établissant le marché commun et les objectifs communs de la Communauté. Leurs importance résulte clairement de l'article 95 (corresponds to article 235 of the EEC Treaty). En autorisant la Haute Autorité à définir les pratiques interdites, le Traité l'oblige à tenir compte de tous les buts prescrits par les articles 2, 3 et 4. Cela découle du renvoi exprès fait au début de l'article 60 auxdits articles".

After this emphasising on the general objectives of the Treaty, the Court continued in a logical way of reasoning based on *literal interpretation* taking the words by their plain meaning and supplemented with the method of taking *account of the context* of a certain word or expression in which it is employed. In this case the Court clarified an expression in article 60 through *comparing the same expression incorporated in another article* and also draw conclusions from the aims of the principle ruling the procedure for publishing pricelists in solving the question of whether the prices in such lists should be precise or not. Considering *the strict wording* of a paragraph and the absence of a text contrary to that the Court drew a conclusion limiting the action of the High Authority. And *ex analogia* the Court held

". . . si le Traité avait voulu . . . ce pouvoir aurait été, en bon logique, subordonné aussi à la consultation du Conseil".

Evidently one can find ways of interpretation used by national as well as international courts. Furthermore, the Court concluded in its final considerations:

"Il reste à examiner si le résultat auquel l'étude des textes et de la ratio legis a amené la Cour n'est pas en opposition avec d'autres objectifs du Traité ou s'il est susceptible d'etre infirmé par d'autres considérations"

which however was not the case, but the statement indicates clearly a certain latitude of argument. In the affirmative event, a re-examination would obviously have been required in order to align the detailed elements to the general objectives of the Treaty but indeed within restricted limits of interpretation, since it did not belong to the Court to pronounce itself upon the

"opportunité du système imposé par le Traité ni de suggérer une révision du Traité"

but only to assure the respect of the law in the interpretation and application of the Treaty

"tel qu'il est établi".

In order to reveal further the Court's development of interpretation a few more examples shall be given. From the affair *Fédération Charbonnière de Belgique versus the High Authority* (R.II:305) one notes the following statements of the Court:

". . . il est permis, sans se livrer à une interprétation extensive, d'appliquer une règle d'interprétation généralement admise tant en droit international qu'en droit national et selon laquelle les normes établies par un traité international ou par une loi impliquent les normes sans lesquelles les premières n'auraient pas de sens ou ne permettraient pas une application raisonnable et utile . . ."

and

"Toutefois, une telle interdiction ne figure pas au texte précité; elle en est déduite par la requérante d'une facon indirecte et a contrario. Or, une telle argumentation n'est admissible qu'en dernier ressort et quand aucune autre interprétation ne s'avère adéquate ou compatible avec le texte, le contexte et leur finalité".

The first section quoted confirms the recognition of implied power (*l'effet utile*); the statements in the case of the *Italian Republic versus the High Authority* (R:VI:665) should not be understood as a denial of the principle of implied power but giving it exactitude, since the Court wrote:

". . . une telle compétence (of the High Authority) étant exceptionelle et subordonnée à une renonciation des États membres qu'en l'espèce le traité ne consacre ni expressément ni implicitement".

The second one expresses the Court's reluctance to apply an *a contrario* interpretation which has been reiterated in subsequent cases.

Further, the *Algera Case* (R.III:118):

"Toute autre interprétation viderait l'article 78 de son contenu et doit partant etre rejetée"

which according to Chevallier, *opus cited,* page 29, is a proof by *reductio ad absurdum* to find the *ratio legis,* provided the authors of the Treaty were reasonable and practical persons.

According to article 53 of the Treaty the High Authority is empowered to undertake certain financial measures pursuant to the procedure established therein for the achievement of the aims defined in article 3 but compatible with the Treaty and in particular with article 65 thereof. The Court held in the case of *Groupement des hauts fourneaux et aciéries belges versus the High Authority* (R.IV:242) that in spite of the express mentioning of article 3, it did not dispense from also taking into account *the rest of the Treaty* (and also annexed instruments) and in particular articles 2, 4, and 5 which had the same force of simultaneous applicability, but however:

"il faudra en pratique procéder à une certaine conciliation entre les divers objectifs de l'article 3, car il est manifestement impossible de les réaliser tous ensemble et chacun au maximum, ces objects étant des principes généraux, vers la réalisation et l'harmonisation desquels il faut tendre dans toute la mesure du possible".

Finally, in the case of *Hoogovens en Staalfabrieken versus the High Authority* (R.XIII:163) the plaintiff had invoked Dutch law in order to elucidate the notion of *proper resources* of the company, but the Court thought one should not link this notion too closely to the national concepts of law, since then one runs the risk, due to the differences between the national laws, of having an ununiform application of community law on the common market.

In the cited decisions of the Court one can find many methods of interpretation represented[4] including the teleological method even though it is modestly and restrictively used, but one finds more of a literal and logical method and context reasoning with regard to objectives of the Treaty which fairly goes along with the rules of interpretation provided for in the *Vienna Convention on the Law of Treaties,* article 31[5]. Later on, however, when the Court felt more familiar with its own role, it abandoned its rather cautious way of argument in favour of a more strong and convincing arrived at by teleological reasoning, see for example the case of *Espérance-Longdoz* (R.XI: 1342):

"le caractère imposable des ferrailles litigieuses découle de l'esprit meme du système de péréquation".

Under the EEC Treaty the Court, from the beginning seems to have felt more free in its approach of interpretation and in using the teleological method of interpretation which appears not only to be explained by the fact that the Court felt more comfortable in its own role but also due to the construction of the Treaties themselves insofar as the EEC Treaty needs to be implemented to a much greater extent which also seems to necessitate other methods of interpretation where the teleological method also appears to be well fitted in considering the conformity of the implementing measures in relation to the declarations proclaimed in the various articles of the Treaty. This method has been employed most frequently by the Court in particular in recent years and one notes for example the following statements:

"... il importe de replacer les articles sus-énoncés dans l'ensemble du traité et de considérer, par rapport aux dispositions fondamentales des articles 2, 3 et 9 et des orientations de l'article 29, le pouvoir que la Commission tient de l'article 25 d'apprécier la légalité et l'opportunité de l'octroi sollicité". *(Germany v. the Commission,* R.IX:141),

"... soulève une difficulté, causée par le silence du nouveau statut ... qu'il appartient donc à la Cour de dégager ... la solution la plus raisonable et la plus susceptible de répondre à la *ratio legis*" (*Colotti v. the Court,* R.X:901),

"... le traité, dont le préambule et le texte visent à supprimer les barrières entre États ..., ne pouvait permettre aux enterprises de recréer de telles barrières" (*Consten and Grundig v. the Commission,* R.XII:494),

"... cet argument doit etre examiné à la lumière tant du texte de l'article 95 que de la nature et de l'esprit du traité instituant la CEE" (*Molkerei v. Hauptzollamt Paderborn,* R.XIV:226), and,

"... il résulte de l'esprit et des finalités du règlement no 974/71 que la décision à cet égard appartient à la Commission et non aux États Membres" (*Merkur v. the Commission,* R.1973:1072).

See also the case of *J C Moulijn v. Commission* (R.1974:1287), when a community text shows language disparities which cannot be reconciled into a clear and uniform meaning, one has to look to its function regarding its aim and general structure, and *Continentale Can Case,* (R.1973:245), consideration 22:

"... l'esprit, l'economie et les termes de l'article 86, compte tenu du système du traité et des finalités qui lui sont propres".

Furthermore, the Court has also used under the Treaties of Tome the literal, context etc. methods, but the intention of the authors of the Treaties have rarely been adduced. This fact seems chiefly due to two reasons. Firstly, the preparatory works have only been fragmentorily published and accordingly do not play a particular important role other than that the Court has assumed that the authors were reasonable and rational men[6]. Secondly, regarding the aims of the Treaties and in particular the EEC it would apparently be contrary to the interests of the intended integration, if the Court had adopted an approach of interpretation purporting to maintain the equilibrium[7] once reached by the authors originating from the "Six" in 1957[8], being more true when the Communities having been enlarged by three new members of which none participated in the deliberations of the Treaties and subsequent implementing legislation until the enlargement. It is consequently not astonishing that the Treaties are living a life of their own[9], and that the starting point of the Court in its interpretation is the sole basis of the Treaties seen in the light of their specific aims and in particular the basic principles set out in the preambles and declarations of principles, but also taking account of, in carrying out the Treaties, the complex interests of the Member-States and their individuals. In elaborating on the aims of the Treaties, this involves taking into account all relevant circumstances, which decides the Court, and being able to comprehend the entire community law in its functioning; one could say that the Court has such a position and ability. One could probably not go any further in explaining what the Court considers about the relevant purpose of community texts.

Emerging from above it is obvious that the Court bears more resemblance to a domestic than an international court regarding its methods of interpretation[10], since, normally, the texts of international treaties are interpreted in a restrictive way under the general presumption that the parties have committed themselves to nothing more, in particular affecting the sovereignty of the contracting states, than what explicitly appears from the texts themselves (which in substance is adopted by the Vienna Convention) other than a reasonable and effective functioning within this limit. Moreover, the Court sometimes goes a little further in particular in preliminary rulings in teleological reasoning than a national court would normally do. In such rulings, due to the separation of functions between the Court (interpreting) and the national courts (applying), the Court's interpretation of community law is in principle performed *in abstracto* free from the circumstances of the actual case. This gives the Court an excellent opportunity to pronounce declarations of principles, although the judgement rendered often leaves in the final end the national court little choice of action.

The conclusion may seem somewhat extraordinary in view of the fact that the Communities doubtlessly belong to international law in the sense of being created by the means of ordinary international treaties, but it is evident that the content of such treaties determine the actual outcome. The situation is clarified through seeing (but in reality the effects are of course reversible) a twofold community[11] with an internal life of its own where community law is the internal law (see Advocate-General Lagrange, R.II:263, and § 3.1) and an external life facing the Community as being a member of the international society where normal public international law applies[12]. However, that an international organisation has its own more or less distinct internal life is in itself nothing extraordinary; note for example the United Nations[13]. That organisation is endowed with an administrative tribunal dealing mainly with employee-disputes but is otherwise referred to use political means as a conflict solution machinery although the General Assembly or the Security Council may request the ICJ to give advisory opinions on legal questions, while the Communities have their Court of Justice as being a *compulsory jurisdiction* with wide competence solving most matters arising within and out of its distinct legal system[14]. Thus the institutions cannot avoid being corrected by the Court in their conduct should

errors occur and also the Member-States as to their failure in their obligations under the Treaties (see art. 169 EEC Treaty). Moreover, features of
public international law in the internal legal order will only be salient to the
extent necessitated with respect to the interstate-relationship of the
Member-States[15], which is in the long run bound to wither away in the
progression of integration but international law will apply to the Communities in the context of the international society, when taking part in international relations, and they may assume liability according to international
law[16].

In the preliminary ruling *International Fruit Company Case* (R.XVIII:1219)
the Court had to examine the compatibility of a community act with the
GATT. The incompatibility of the community act with a rule of international
law could only affect the validity of the act concerned, if
1) the international rule bound the Community and 2) the interested party
could avail himself of that rule before national jurisdiction (i.e. a self-executing rule). The Court took the same view in the *Schlüter Case*[17] but found in
no case the second criterion to be satisfied. As to the first criterion international agreements concluded by a Community will of course be binding upon
that Community, agreements concluded by the Member-States in such fields
where the Community has assumed responsibility as an effect of the transfer
of national competency upon the Community by the Treaty (see *International
Fruit Company Case,* R.XVIII:1228, consideration 18) and probably also other
rules in public international law, e.g. concerning the good order in the
international society. The second criterion means evidently a limitation for
indivduals to contest community acts. In order to find out whether individuals are able to refer to a rule of international law in contesting a community act, the Court stated:

"il convient d'envisager à la fois, l'esprit, l'économie et les termes de l'Accord
Général".

This second criterion seems, however, not to exclude an individual from
invoking a breach of an international rule of law binding the Community *in
proceedings instituted before the Court,* e.g. in an action for indemnity; cf. the
Haegeman Cases (R.XVIII:1005 and R.1974:459), which concerned an
international agreement concluded by the EEC.

Finally, one should note some provisions in articles 233, which concern
the Benelux-union, and 234 of the EEC Treaty dealing with international
conventions concluded between one or more Member-States and third
states. Although the Treaty does not contain any provisions as to the position
of treaties concluded subsequent to the coming into force of the EEC Treaty,
one may understand from the aforementioned articles compared with article
5 that the Member-States are not allowed to circumvent the Treaty by
conventions concluded either between themselves or, with third states[18].

Such agreements will generally from the Court's view assume the same position as national legislation, and the validity of a community act will not be affected should it violate such an agreement[19]. Note, however, that the Court can be asked by the Commission, the Council or a Member-State whether an intended convention is in conformity with the Treaty and subsequent community law.

One should also note that the Court has emphasised the distinction between community decisions and international agreements (*Commission v. Italy*, R.XVI:57).

The notable thing regarding the community legal system is that the Member-States are actually in a supranational manner — within the area determined by the Treaty — together with the individuals in their states subjected to community law[20] of which many rules have the character of being self-executing[21]. The community law has the characteristics in relation to national law of being autonomous, supreme and in particular regulations being directly applicable, which the Court has always emphasised in its judgements[22] in order to ensure the full effectiveness of community law. This viewpoint is now widespreadly accepted by national courts, which contributes to the same force of applicability in all the Member-States[23], although there are set-backs[24]. The willingness by national courts to adhere to the community rules is also reflected by the increased number of preliminary rulings referred to the Court mostly concerning conflicts between an individual and a national authority which undoubtedly gives the Court a decisive sway over the national courts and indirectly also over the Member-States' international behaviour. However, the recognition of the primacy and the direct applicability of community law can be done differently according to the nature of the community act[25] and with regard to the national law concerned; this involves many delicate problems which can not be dealt with here, but the general tendency is according to the Commission's seventh general report (1973) that community law is gaining force in penetration on the national level.

However, it seems proper to return to the judgement of the German *Bundesverfassungsgericht* mentioned in footnote 24 which reveals the question of community law in relation to the constitutional laws of the Member-States. In this context Germany and Italy attract special attention, since they have constitutional courts examining the constitutionality of legislative acts. In a decision of October 18, 1967, the Constitutional Court of Germany stated it could not review the legality of community acts (*CMLReview 1967—68*, p. 483—484), though the question was left open as to reviews relating to fundamental rights expressed in the constitution[26]. In its judgement of May 29, 1974, the *Bundesverfassungsgericht* pronounced (translation in *Common Market Law Reports 1974*, p. 540 f) that it will determine "the inapplicability (not the nullity) of a rule of Community law by the administrative or judicial authorities in so far as it conflicts with a guarantee of fundamental rights in the Constitution"

as long as

"the Community itself lacks any codified Bill of Rights and a democratically legitimated parliament to which the Community legislative organs are fully responsible on a political level".

The community organs are not competent in principle directly to apply any kind of national legislation, and in e.g. the *Stork Case* (R.V:63) the Court did not pay any attention to the invocation of the alleged infringement of the German constitutional law by community law. However, during recent years the Court has taken account of fundamental rights. One notes here three cases.

In the *Stauder Case* (R.XV:425) the Court solved the issue by means of interpretation and stated:

"qu'ainsi interprétée, la disposition litigieuse ne révèle aucun élément susceptible de mettre en cause les droits fondamentaux de la personne compris dans les principes généraux du droit communautaire, dont la Cour assure le respect".

The case of *Internationale Handelsgesellschaft mbH versus the Einfuhr- und Vorratstelle für Getreide und Futtermittel* (R.XVI:1135):

"... que la validité de tel actes (community acts) ne sauraient etre appréciée qu'en fonction du droit communautaire; ... que, dès lors, l'invocation d'atteintes portées, soit aux droits fondamentaux tels qu'ils sont formulés par la constitution d'un État membre, soit aux principes d'une structure constitutionelle nationale, ne saurait affecter la validité d'un acte de la Communauté ou son effet sur le territoire de cet État; attendu qu'il convient toutefois d'examiner si aucune garantie analogue, inhérente au droit communautaire, n'aurait été méconnue; qu'en effet, le respect des droits fondamentaux fait partie intégrante des principes généraux du droit dont la Cour de justice assure le respect; que la sauvegarde de ces droits, tout en s'inspirant des traditions constitutionnelles communes aux États membres, doit etre assurée dans le cadre de la structure et des objectifs de la Communauté".

The Court held in the case of *Nold* (R.1974:508):

"qu'en assurant la sauvegarde de ces droits, la Cour est tenue de s'inspirer des traditions constitutionelles communes aux États membres et ne saurait, dès lors, admettre des mesures incompatibles avec les droits fondamentaux reconnus et garantis par les Constitutions de ces États; que les instruments internationaux concernant la protection des droits de l'homme auxquels les États membres ont coopéré ou adhéré peuvent également fournir des indications dont il convient de tenir compte dans le cadre du droit communautaire".

However, the Court thought limitations could be imposed on these rights when justified by the aims of general interest pursued by the Community. This implies that community rules claim to prevail before the constitutional rules in the Member-States and the judicial protection involved therein is, however, substitued by general principles of law related to rules normally incorporated in the constitutions of the Member-States and guidance may also be obtained from the European Convention on Human Rights. It appears from the last section quoted from the *Nold Case* that the Court had not taken account of the fact that France a few days before the judgement had ratified the Convention on Human Rights, and therefore it is uncertain whether the Court had considered the EEC to be bound by the Convention as it did with the GATT, if account of that fact had been taken. Now the Court followed the approach from the *Interfood Case* (R.XVIII:243) in which it stated that the GATT could *assist* in the interpretation of the Common Customs Tariff.

Chevallier wrote in the *Common Market Law Review 1964,* (p. 35):

"one can conclude that the Court is at the same time an international and a court whose techniques of interpretation tend more and more to resemble those of a national court and this without the court ever going beyond the limits assigned to it by the jurisdiction-conferring clause of the treaties".

This is a statement which one may perhaps place in doubt today regarding the last sentence[27] and which is of course clearly related to one's own opinion of the Communities specifically and of European integration generally. In referring to article 4 of the EEC Treaty it is evident that the Court, together with the other institutions, shall strive to achieve the objectives of the Treaty, and undoubtedly also to promote the Communities' cause. But the means of the Court differ from those of the other institutions, since the Court shall safeguard the integration procedure so it is performed legally i.e. under the legal standards of community law, which however afford a certain scope for action. The limits the Court cannot exceed in interpreting and applying the Treaties and subsequent legislation seem then to be that its interpretation is generally accepted by the various subjects concerned, even though the teleological method might sometimes lead to an extension of the text. To end this paragraph it seems proper to cite a few words from Pescatore[28]:

"It is in the light of such concepts (previously mentioned as economic interpenetration, unity of the market, free circulation etc. viewed in connection with fundamental provisions of the Treaties) that the scope of the Treaties can be clarified, that competences can be defined, exceptions circumscribed, and gaps filled in the light of a coherent purpose".

§ 9.2 The general principles common to the laws of the Member-States

Thus bearing in mind the position of the Court and its general approach in the interpretation and application of community law it is now suitable to proceed to a closer examination of the common principles referred to in articles 215 (2) and 188 (2) of the EEC and EAEC Treaties respectively appearing more or less as a choice-of-law clause, not to one or two specified national legal systems but to principles common to nine different legal orders; the articles concerned give also criteria as to institutions, performance of duties etc., which have previously been dealt with, but leave the rest to be found out by means of those common principles. Furthermore, the situation presenting itself to the Court in applying the Rome Treaties on this subject was indeed the already delivered judgements under the ECSC Treaty on the basis of *faute de service*. From Chapters five, six, seven and eight the actual results that the Court has arrived at in applying the aforementioned articles in solving concrete disputes brought before it may be seen. It is now the purpose of the forthcoming description to reveal the ways of reasoning by the Court in interpreting these articles and arriving at these actual results. Through the evolution of the case-law relating to the non-contractual liability of the EEC the action for indemnity has acquired its own specific concepts and independent character within the community legal framework.

The reference to common principles could be comprehended in different ways. According to Stein and Hay in *AJCL 1960,* page 420 these common principles referred to in article 215 (2) are said to be reminiscent of the general principles of law of article 38 (1) (c) of the statute of the ICJ. It often occurs in agreements on the international level that references are made to general principles of law, for example in contracts between a state of a developing country and a private company but also frequently in agreements concluded by international organisations; the United Nations Administrative Tribunal looks for example to such principles of the member states in supplementing staff-regulations. A reference to general principles of law recognised by the civilised nations has in practice often turned out to be good faith, acquired rights, unjust enrichment, *pacta sunt servanda*[29] etc. and it is quite natural that one should find such coherence in the legal thinking on a high level of abstraction but such principles are obviously not always detailed enough to offer rules in order to solve concrete problems, since one knows, for example, that *enrichissement sans cause* has not been endowed the same content and field of application in all states of the world recognising such a principle; it is thus clear that if one adopts a perspective large enough and arrives at a level of high abstraction, it is accordingly not astonishing that one will find common principles since, after all, all rules of law concern activities of human-beings. The wording in article 38 (1) (c) *recognised by civilised nations* also raises (note the word *all* before nations is missing) the problem of the criteria for a civilised nation and further how many of them should be required to subscribe to a certain principle to constitute it as a general one, which is a problem that becomes more important the lower level of abstraction employed. It has been suggested that it should not only concern a minority of states, Lorenz says[30] but a greater part, and perhaps it may be sufficient, if the most influential countries in legal thinking sustain a principle provided no opposition against it is lodged[31]. A general principle of law is according to Mann[32] constituted when it is applied by the most representative systems of municipal law.

The reference to general principles of law serves, however, rather often as a diplomatic formula empowering a judge (arbitrator) to find a fair and acceptable solution taking into consideration the specific circumstances in the particular dispute without any profound enquiry into various legal systems in order to find out how the principle adduced actually is applied. It is hard to conceive that such an indefinite meaning should be attributed to article 215 (2), as regards principles, in considering the order, legal security and systematics of the Treaty and the same manner in which the Court applies community law; such an interpretation and application of article 215 (2) must therefore be rejected.

However, one could, on the other hand, proceed to a substantial comparative study with the concrete problem as the starting point and then note the outcome in different domestic systems and through that discover a common basis[33]; in such an approach one could not of course pay any importance to whether the legal rules are to be characterised as belonging to public or private law or be bound by any other domestic classification[34]. Here also one could work on different levels of abstraction and concerning non-contractual state liability it would not help very much in saying that such a liability exists in all Member-States in order to solve the very concrete problems of an actual case before the Court, but one must proceed to a more thorough study involving to a greater extent details of the various systems and at such a level the discrepancies will also become apparent between the systems. Finding common principles to all Member-States on that level tends indeed to be a procedure of ascertaining the minidenominator consisting of almost identical rules to be applied[35] and thus favouring the less developed legal system, which is an approach overwhelmingly rejected by the writers in the doctrine[36], and, besides, as Lecheler[37] indicated, although two rules are identical this does not imply that they are sustained by the same legal thinking. This is perfectly true, since firstly it appears nowadays from the case-law that the Court as a matter of fact has not been looking for the minidenominator, secondly it would be contrary to the flexible approach of the Court and impede it from taking account of community needs in the context of the structure and aims of the Treaties and community law as a whole. However, comparative studies seem to be very important to the Court, although the Court very seldom (e.g. the *Algera Case*, R.III:115) invokes such studies in its judgements and has indeed never done so concerning the terms of non-contractual liability, but the Advocates-General have instead frequently provided the Court with sometimes exhaustive studies when pertinent. Furthermore, the parties before the Court often invoke national principles in order to support their arguments. It is then urgent to consider the interplay between the Advocates-General deliveries of those studies and the actual reasoning of the Court in its judgements in comprehending the role of comparative studies and thus also in what manner the national laws of the Member-States serve as a source of inspiration to the Court. It may be interesting incidently to note an event from the ECSC Treaty. The system of *faute de service* was accorded by the Treaty itself and was taken from the French system, and thus already having a characteristic substance from that national system, but the Court has simultaneoulsy through comparative surveys of the national systems (e.g. *Feram Case*, R.V:525f) provided by the Advocates-General, the context of the Treaty and also the reasoning relating to community circumstances, conveyed the notion of a community significance and has accordingly not clinged narrowly to concepts of the French law[38]. Advocate-General Roemer took the view in the *Plaumann Case* that useful guidance could be obtained from the caselaw of the ECSC to be applied to the EEC Treaty, but depending on the circumstances in that case the Court did not pronounce itself on that matter. In the next case raising the item of non-contractual liability of the EEC (*Kampffmeyer Case*, R.XIII:352f) Advocate-General Gand considered as a general principle of law the fact that public administrations assumed liability in all the Member-States as well as one finds in all such systems three basic elements namely, an incriminating fact, a damage and a causal link between these facts, which the Court also adopted and labelled the basis for liability to be *faute de service*.

Thus having easily established the basic ideas the case-law has revealed two questions within the action for indemnity which have not been so easy to solve: 1) the necessity of the annulment of the act alleged to have caused the damage as a prerequisite to the action for indemnity and 2) a possible liability resulting from illegal normative acts, of which both issues were solved in regard to national solutions put into the context of the Treaty and of the community structure itself. The Advocate-General Roemer had to deal with both items in the *Schöppenstedt Case* (R.XVII:990) where he started to examine the item number two putting forward the following arguments. In referring to comparative studies made by the Max-Planck Institute[39] he found that at least in France and Belgium normative legislative acts could give rise to indemnity for damage caused and one could nor exclude such liability in Germany and Italy although the techniques and means were different. These statements were sufficient in conceiving article 215, since one should not interpret it in a too literal manner, and the community law could not exclusively consider rules prevailing in all Member-States, which would be a recognition of the minidenominator, but one should proceed critically in taking account of the aims of the Treaty and the community structure; perhaps one should also take as a guide-mark the most developed (elaborated) national law. He also took account of the insufficient parliamentary control in the Community, article 34 in the ECSC Treaty by which it is possible to repair damage resulting from annulled general decisions i.e. a normative act, and articles 177 and 184 of the EEC Treaty granting to individuals the possibility to contest incidently normative acts; however, in spite of the liberal interpretation of the Court regarding the access to these latter means, they were not always available. Therefore normative acts could be invoked in actions for indemnity.

From these considerations Advocate-General Roemer turned to the issue of the necessity that the contested act should have been annulled earlier (primarily revealed by the *Plaumann Case*), which is a delicate problem from the point of view that serious problems may occur when it turns out several years later to the issue of the act that the whole act or parts of it are illegal, although the administration is not compelled to follow the procedure in article 176 (1). Nevertheless, the Advocate-General Roemer did not think the annulment was a necessary prerequisite and regarding this issue put forward the following arguments exposing as well four different sources of law:

1) Article 34 of the ECSC Treaty expressly provided for
"la décision ou de la recommandation annulée"
while the EEC Treaty did not (written community law);
2) A comparative study showed that French, Belgian and German law did not require a declaration of the illegality nor an annulment previous to the action for indemnity. As for the other Member-States not being familiar with such a solution that seemed to depend on the lack of competency of the ordinary courts in actions for indemnity to state upon the illegality of administrative acts (recourse to national laws);
3) Authors in the doctrine had strongly criticised the *Plaumann Case* (cf. the Statute of the International Court article 38);
4) The structure of the Treaty itself with regard to the use of article 177 allowed an individual to obtain the establishment of the alleged illegality but he would then lose time by which the time limit in article 43 of the Statute of the Court may have expired; furthermore the occurrance of the damage after the time limit for an action for annulment would empty the same article in the Statute of its content (community law), and
5) The Court had expressed itself (*Lütticke Case*) in favour of the action for indemnity as being an autonomous and particular action (community case-law).

The further conclusions presented to the Court were that the action for indemnity was an action of its own and subordinate *inter alia* to the illegality of the contested act and to the existence of a committed fault. The Court allowed the invocation of a non-annulled normative act in an action for indemnity, which could give cause to liability provided the existence, due to article 215 (2), of a sufficiently characterised breach of a superior rule of law protecting the individuals.

The procedure thus to be followed in finding and incorporating into community law general principles common to the laws of the Member-States is:

1) what do the laws of the Member-States tell pertaining to the item in hand, where the general attitude of the national laws is to be sought;
2) what in particular has the most judicially developed system to tell;
3) what are the pecularities in the community system to be considered;
4) could the attitude to solutions by the laws of the Member-States be adapted into the community system having regard also to the aims of the Treaty and other relevant community legislation.

However, there is one item relating to points one and two which must be developed further while the other considerations will find their proper application in their actual context. Thus one notes, on the one hand, that the notion of *faute de service* has been incorporated into the community system from the French system, and, on the other hand, that the question of the admissibility of invoking a normative act as generating the damage in an action for indemnity is beyond doubt permissible in at least *two* states, but yet the Court in allowing the admissibility of such acts had to add a qualification (sufficiently characterised breach of a superior rule of law protecting the individuals) in referring to article 215 (2) which evidently indicates the account of the positions in *all* Member-States. One could conceive this reasoning of the Court as a tightening up of the interpretation of article 215 (2) but also another explanation emerges, which, however, appears more feasible. *Faute de service* is certainly a French notion, and it seems clear furthermore, that the French system of state liability from a legal and technical viewpoint is the most developed, since it has been separate from the civil system for several years with the purpose of being shaped to meet the peculiar needs of state liability. The notion nevertheless covers a reality familiar to all Member-States' systems insofar as some kind of culpability on behalf of the administration is needed to add to the damaging fact but the means and the extent of the actual liability differ. Since the notion allows a flexible application which is indeed suitable for community purposes as the community is being constantly submitted to conditions of development, the Court adopted it, and placed it in a community context but the concerns of the other states are taken into consideration with respect to the actual application of the notion in thus maintaining a balance as to the positions of the national laws. This balance was also attained when admitting normative acts to be invoked, a procedure not known to all states, through restrictions being introduced when adopting this possibility into the community context.

The principle that a violation of a rule of law intended for the protection of the individuals must have occurred in certain instances has a rather feeble basis, since it is mainly applied in Germany but is furthermore not unknown to the Belgian and Italian systems. However, it might be seen as a balancing measure within the framework of the community liability system. Evidently the elements taken from the national systems form a synthesis where the community liability system to a substantial part links up with the spirit of each national system; furthermore, the Advocate-General Roemer said in the *Plaumann Case* (R.IX:241) that although the means and technics differed in the various state in solving a problem, it appeared that "les résultats coincident pourtant en gros".

The positions of all the Member-States are counted insofar as they are always balanced, and from that process emerges judge-made community law[40]. There is an element of progression involved in the approach adopted by the Court, since the Court is able to draw the advantages from the most developed system in placing that system ahead.

The reference to article 215 (2) in the judgements indicates that the Court feels a certain limitation in the reception of national law; however, since there are no provisions which bind the Court outside article 215 (2) there is no formal hindrance to the Court in adopting a solution peculiar to a certain country without being balanced. The Court has in dealing with the Treaties in general primarily been inspired by the various national systems, and one notes for example the evolution of *détournement de pouvoir* under ECSC Treaty although there are no express reference to national laws or any other source of law to be applied. In article 33 of the ECSC Treaty there are four grounds for illegality exactly corresponding to the ones of the French *Conseil d'État* among which *détournement de pouvoir* is one, and furthermore, the single language of the Treaty is also French; the question was whether the Court should cling to the French concept considering the impact of French connections and disregard the differences in relation to the German *Ermessenmissbrauch,* the Italian *sviamento di potere* and the Dutch *misbruik van bevoegdheid* or not; the Court did not, but alloted to the original French version a broader concept influenced by the aforementioned laws and thus also a peculiar community meaning not identical to any of the national laws. See further W Lorenz in *AJCL 1964,* page 9 f and there made references. Furthermore, the very composition of the Court, i.e. the fact that the judges are gathered from all Member-States, ensures by itself that national solutions will not be disregarded, nor will a single national system solely be applied. According to Pescatore[41] the collegial character of the Court is salient and the working-system is said to favour a spirit of synthesis. Indeed this conclusion emerges; therefore, there seems to be no difference in the procedure concerning the reception of the national laws of the Member-States as to whether it takes place within the applications of article 215 (2) or not. Finally, to what extent an adopted solution should be balanced, is a question to which one can only answer, to the extent necessary for it to be generally accepted[42].

In the case of *Werhahn* (R.1973:1271) the Advocate-General Roemer considered an invoked principle to be unknown to international law, and it could therefore not be admitted as a general principle of law in the meaning of article 215 (2). This consideration reveals whether "the *laws* of the Member-States" in article 215 (2) include, besides domestic law of the Member-States, international law binding or has been recognised by them[43]. Furthermore, the consideration of international law also concerns the positions of that law in the Member-States. In spite of all difficult and complex questions in this respect, one may perhaps presume provided international law should at all be included in article 215 (2), that a rule in international law which is commonly recognised by the Member-States or a rule contained in a treaty ratified by all Member-States could be embodied by article 215 (2), but on occasions when one or more Member-States expressly has made objections to a rule in international law or not ratified a treaty one could perhaps employ the same procedure as done to domestic laws.

§ 9.3 Present system and future developments

To summarise, the system of the Rome Treaties relating to non-contractual liability is based on the notion of *faute de service*. This implies that the administration has committed a damaging action which is due to a sufficient amount of culpability incurring liability. The action giving cause to liability may consist of any mistake; in particular one notes illegal acts committed by a positive action as well as an omission. The illegalities are established according to the grounds in article 173 of the EEC Treaty. Here one notes the third ground for the Court of reviewing the legality of an act, namely the
"infringement of this Treaty or *any rule of law relating to its application*",
which should be read together with article 164 stating that the Court ensures in the interpretation and application of this Treaty the law is observed. The Court has several times pronounced that it ensures the respect for general principles of law or general principles of community law. Those general principles of law consist of general principles common to the laws of the Member-States and principles in international law provided they relate to the application of the Treaty. Those principles form accordingly the unwritten community law[44], which as well can be invoked to have been violated by a community act and form the basis for an action for indemnity. There shall also exist a damage, and between this and the damaging fact there shall be a

direct link of cause. It is also required that the action of the administration should have violated a rule destined to protect the interest of the injured party, which sometimes is necessary in connection with illegalities. Regarding liability resulting from normative acts, it is additionally required that the illegality should imply a sufficiently serious breach of a major rule of law protecting the individuals.

The above-mentioned rules had been elaborated by the Court before entrance of the new Member-States, and it is thus pertinent to ask the question whether the laws of the new Member-States have had or will have any influence on the thinking of the Court as to a modification of the present system.

These issues were touched upon by the Advocate-General Roemer in the case of *Werhahn* (R.1973:1257) in the context of the admissibility of individuals to invoke normative acts, since the Council and the Commission once more sustained the inadmissibility which was based *inter alia* on arguments drawn from taking account of the legal positions in the new Member-States in that respect. However, the Advocate-General Roemer took the view that there was no reason to change the present system in setting forward the following considerations:

1) the principle concerned was already adopted and belonged to community law before the adherence of the new Members and had been accepted by the adhering states as a matter of course[45];

2) it was doubtful furthermore whether the laws of the new Members should be taken into consideration at all, since the facts involved and alleged to have generated the damage were related to circumstances occurring before the adherence of the new Members to the Communities;

3) even though account was taken of the laws in the three new states relating to the issue concerned, and one could not from them confirm the rule adopted nevertheless it seemed unnecessary to change the rules adopted, since one should look to the balanced effect of the various laws and not with the purpose of seeking the consent of all laws, besides, one could see a tendency in the three new states towards an improvement in this respect;

4) one should consider the specific community structure which obviously was not the same as that of a state, e.g. with regard to the legislative power of the British Parliament compared with the Council or the Commission. In the community structure it was the task of the Court to re-enforce the legal protection accorded by community law.

The Court maintained its earlier adopted rule but the judgement does not reveal what argument was decisive to the Court in its thinking; the arguments put forward by the Advocate-General are convincing and in particular in that case. Looking towards the future in considering general terms it appears perfectly feasible that the Court will maintain its adopted system as long as it serves community purposes. As to the effects of the enlargement of the Communities, although the present relatively restrictive status of the new Members pertaining to state liability, it seems nevertheless to exist a tendency implying it has become easier to obtain indemnity from the Communities, which breaks up the Court's rather restrictive attitude in that respect; to that end one notes the cases of *Holtz & Willemsen, Compagnie Continentale,* and *CNTA.* Furthermore, one can perceive the possibility of reconsiderations as to the position of *faute de service,* which has already been indicated in § 5.2. It appears also that the thinking of the Court inevitably as a matter of course will be influenced by the legal thinking of the three new Member-States that gradually will grow in importance until some kind of balance is reached. However, it would seem that the community purposes will generally override the influence of the national laws, if the question is put at its edge.

Finally, it is to consider the possible developments of liability for damaging actions not connected with a fault within the community liability system while what concerns the case-law in that respect has been revealed in §§ 8.2 and 8.3 relating to the ECSC and EEC Treaties. It remains then to consider whether the activities of the Communities in general — except nuclear — might incur the liability of the Communities, that is to say whether such a principle might be encompassed by articles 215 (2) the EEC Treaty and 188 (2) the EAEC Treaty.

In the *Werhahn Case* (p. 1274) the Advocate-General thought that the basis of consent by the laws of the Member-States concerning the invoked German concept was too weak to be applied as a general principle in the sense of article 215 (2) particularly since considerable differences appeared between the national systems in this field of law. He also thought that the *First Spaak Report* supported the exclusion of such a liability, since one from that report could draw the conclusion that the authors of the Treaties had intended to exclude compensation resulting from inconveniences related to the implementation of the Treaties, since otherwise it would entail inflexibility as to economic policies and restructural measures which were also said to be supported by the economy of the EEC Treaty itself. However, the French system of equality concerning public charges seems never to have hampered the French government from taking proper economic measures when necessary. Furthermore, considering the Court's approach of interpretation the authors of the Treaties have rarely been invoked in support of a certain interpretation but rather the spirit of the Treaty, its structure, purposes etc. (see § 9.1). It is obvious that the Treaty is living its own and intended eternal life; in such circumstances the needs of the Community must necessarily change according to the times in and adaptations must be made which has also been ensured by the powers endowed to the Council in article 235 in order to achieve the objectives of the EEC Treaty at any time[46].

One could thus argue the point of the compatibility with the Treaty in adopting a rule giving liability for damaging actions without fault from the viewpoint of the aims, structure etc. of the Treaty but in the moment the Court considered such a protection to be in conformity with the Treaty in general, the question which remains to be answered is whether it would be in conformity with the meaning of article 215 (2) as such.

It has been pointed out in § 9.2 one has not to seek consent from all the laws of the Member-States on a specific principle nor is there a need to quote a ratio between approving or disapproving states of a principle but it concerns converging ideas and trends on a higher legal level. It appears from the general survey of the laws of the Member-States with regard to objective liability in general that *all* nine states indeed recognise such a liability but to different extents and by different means and mainly applied in the field of public works and situations where private persons (e.g. dangerous activities) are held liable; only in France and Belgium and perhaps also in Denmark and Germany could one speak of a liability resulting from legal actions. This basis seems in several aspects to be weaker than the basis of normative acts generating damage but still one cannot exclude that the existing basis might be sufficient for the Court in recognising such a liability in cases of obvious injustice which thus also will contribute to an increased legal protection which appears essential in a society characterised by increased public interference in the lives of private persons. From the *CIE Case* it appears that before the enlargement of the Communities the Court was not reluctant to consider an eventual indemnity resulting from a legal act (curiously enough not considered by the Advocate-General in the *Werhahn Case*). Furthermore, one notes that the Court employed the French concepts in this area of law; whether the Court will maintain this approach according to the French concepts as a framework for further development is hard at present to tell in particular considering the laws of the new Member-States. But as already indicated in § 8.3 the French system seems to grant a sufficient amount of flexibility which would easily imply an adaptation to community purposes and also having due regard to the developments of the laws of *all* Member-States. Here also, in a short perspective, the decisive element will be what the Court thinks is acceptable and what will be accepted, it seems however, that the Community would not lose anything in granting this legal protection but on the contrary.

Footnotes chapter nine

1. See *inter alia:* Stein and Hay in *AJCL 1960*, p. 420 f, L T Løddesøl *TfR 1963*, pp. 335—341, R-M Chevallier in *CMLReview 1964*, pp. 21—35, P Pescatore in *CMLReview 1970*, pp. 167—183, J F McMahon in *BYIL 1961*, pp. 320—350, P Reuter in *Mélanges offerts à Henri Rolin*, pp. 263—283, R. Monaco in *Mélanges offerts à Henri Rolin*, pp. 218—227, P Pescatore in collaboration with A Donner, R Monaco and H Kutscher

in *ZaöRVR 32 (1972)*, pp. 239—252, H Baade in *Essays in honour of Robert R Wilson*, pp. 19—39, F Rigaux in *Miscellanea W J Ganshof van der Meersch*, pp. 365—381, M R Mok in *CMLReview 1971*, pp. 485—494, P Pescatore in *Miscellanea W J Ganshof van der Meersch*, pp. 325—363, F Aubert in *Revue trimestrielle de droit Européen 1966*, pp. 729—751, R Lecourt, Le juge devant le Marché Commun, *L'Institute Universitaire des Hautes études*, pp. 5—69 and P Pescatore *Legal problems of an enlarged EC*, pp. 27—46, P Pescatore, *L'ordre juridique des Communautés Européennes*, I Brownlie, *Principles of public international law*, pp. 604—613.

2. For a general outline see Part I and in particular Chapter three.

3. Note that in preliminary rulings pursuant to article 177 EEC Treaty, the parties, the Member-States, the Commission and, where appropriate, the Council may submit statements or written observations concerning the case pending before the Court (art. 20 of the EEC Statute of the Court). The Commission uses this possibility very often.

4. The Court has interpreted the ECSC Treaty in referring to the EEC:
"si on admet une communauté d'inspiration entre les articles 65 du traité CECA et 85 du traité CEE",

Comptoir de Vente de Charbon de la Ruhr v. High Authority, R.VIII:201. Also language comparison has been employed, *Hoogovens v. High Authority*, R.XIII:289.

5. Article 31 reads:
"General rules of interpretation
1. A treaty shall be interpreted in good faith in accordance with the ordinary meaning to be given to the terms of the treaty in their context and in the light of its object and purpose.
2. The context for the purpose of the interpretation of a treaty shall comprise, in addition to the text, including its preamble and annexes . . ."

and also other instruments relating to the treaty, subsequent practice and rules of international law applicable to the parties' relations.

Article 32 reads *in extenso:*
"Supplementary means of interpretation
Recourses may be had to supplementary means of interpretation, including the preparatory work of the treaty and the circumstances of its conclusion, in order to confirm the meaning resulting from the application of article 31, or to determine the meaning when the interpretation according to article 31:
a) leaves the meaning ambiguous or obscure; or
b) leads to a result which is manifestly absurd or unreasonable."

Brownlie states, *opus cited*, p. 610, in commenting upon article 32:
"Somewhat distinct from this procedure is the more radical teleological approach according to which a court determines what the objects and purposes are and then resolves any ambiguity of meaning by importing the substance 'necessary' to give effect to the purposes of the treaty. This may involve a judicial implementation of purposes in a fashion not contemplated in fact by the parties. At the same time the textual approach in practice often leaves the decision maker with a choice of possible meanings and in exercising that choice it is impossible to keep considerations of policy out of account. Many issues of interpretation are by no means narrow technical enquiries."

In all instances when dealing with general objectives, it seems unavoidable to interpret them, which will be affected by the interpreter's own political views; sometimes, one cannot escape the impression that the adoption of a special technic of interpretation serves the purpose of covering up an already prejudged opinion. See concerning the interpretation of treaties in general A D McNair, *The law of treaties*, pp. 364—473, L Delbez, *Les principes généraux du droit international public*, pp. 347—350, and Brownlie, *opus cited*, pp. 604—611.

6. Note e.g. *Commission v. Italy*, R.VIII:21:
"elle permet d'en conclure que les auteurs du traité se sont rendu compte de la différence . . .".

7. See P Pescatore, *CMLReview 1970*, p. 174.

8. *Molkerei Westfalen Case*, R.XIV:226:
". . . que l'objectif du traité CEE, . . . implique que ce traité constitue plus qu'un accord qui ne créerait que des obligations mutuelles entre les États contractants".

9. McMahon in *BYIL 1961*, p. 323 and 349.

10. See R-M Chevallier, *opus cited*, p. 35, J F McMahon, *opus cited*, p. 329, R Monaco, *opus cited*, p. 221, P Pescatore in *ZaöRVR*, p. 240.
The fact that the Court is more alike a national court than an international as to its methods of interpretation is further due to the fact that the major part of the cases brought before it concerns matters typical for a national court which makes the frequent resorts to national laws natural and evidently also affects the methods of interpretation employed.

11. See P Pescatore in *CMLReview 1970*, pp. 168—170.

12. See on the external and internal competency of the Communities the case of *Commission versus Council* (R.XVII:263) and also the subsequent comments upon the case by J-V Louis in *Cahiers 1971*, pp. 479—490.

13. See J F McMahon in *BYIL 1961*, p. 320.
14. *W. Wilhelm v. Bundeskartellamt*, R.XV:15:

". . . que le traité CEE a institué un ordre juridique propre, intégré au système juridique des États Membres et qui s'impose à leurs juridictions".

15. See *van Duyn Case*, R.1974:1352, consideration 22:
"que, d'autre part, un principe de droit international, que le traité CEE ne peut pas etre censé méconnaitre dans les rapports entre les États membres, s'oppose à ce qu'un État refuse à ses propres ressortissant le droit d'avoir accès à son territoire et d'y séjourner".

However, international law will not always be possible to invoke but the special nature of the Treaties will intermingle. Thus in the case of the *Commission v. Belgium and Luxembourg* (R.X:1231f) the defendants had invoked international law but the Court held:
"que le droit international reconnaissant, selon eux, à la partie lésée par l'inexécution des obligations incombant à une autre partie, le droit de se dispenser de l'exécution des siennes . . . attendu toutefois que ce lien entre les obligationes des sujets ne saurait etre reconnu dans le cadre du droit communautaire",

since the Treaty did not limit itself to create reciprocal obligations but established a new legal order regulating powers, rights and obligations between the Member-States.

16. In the event that a third state feels concerned over a considered breach of public international law by a Community, there exists, it would seem, only one remedy, namely to enter into diplomatic negotiations with that Community, since one probably cannot refer to the International Court of Justice, when article 34 of its Statute is concerned only with states, and the Communities do not yet at least form a state. However, a special agreement between the parties may change the situation. Note also that the conditions for liability in public international law differ from that within the Communities; see to that end I Brownlie, *opus cited*, p. 423 f, L Delbez, *opus cited*, p. 350 f and M Green, *International Law*, p. 243 f.

17. R.1973:1157:
". . . que la validité, au sens de l'article 177 du traité, des actes pris par les institutions ne peut etre appréciée au regard d'une disposition du droit international que si cette disposition lie la Communauté et est de nature à engendrer, pour les justiciable, le droit de s'en prévaloir en justice".

H Schermers, *CMLReview 1975,* p. 80 f criticised the second condition mainly on the basis that a court should apply its binding rules of law but thought that the reason may have been pragmatic.

"Under international law many States undertake obligations which they never execute in their national legal orders and most States do not accept any direct applicability".

If the Court enforced the Community's obligations, the Community would be in an unequal situation regarding its international relations, which is now avoided by classifying the majority of international rules as not being self-executing. Not would only the Community be in an unequal position but also the Member-States, which probably has been the main concern in the cases dealing with the GATT.

18. In the case of *Commission versus Italy* (R.VIII:22) the Court pronounced:

"qu'en effet le traité CEE prime, dans les matières qu'il règle, les conventions conclues avant son entrée en vigueur entre les États membres, y compris les conventions intervenues dans le cadre du GATT".

Note also a statement made by the Court concerning the competency of concluding international agreements in the *Commission versus the Council Case,* R.XVII:274, consideration 17,

"qu'en particulier, chaque fois que, pour la mise en oeuvre d'une politique commune prévue par le traité, la Communauté a pris des dispositions instaurant, sous quelque forme que ce soit, des règles communes, les États membres ne sont plus en droit, qu'ils agissent individuellement ou meme collectivement, de contracter avec les États tiers des obligations affectant ces règles".

19. In the *Vandeweghe Case* (R.1973:1329) the Court held, it had no competency in preliminary rulings to interpret international law binding the Member-States outside the framework of community law. Here it concerned a bilateral agreement between Belgium and Germany from 1957 in which there was no prorogation clause giving competence to the Court according to article 182 of the EEC Treaty, which otherwise would have applied. In the *Haegeman Case* (R.1974:459) the Court stated that it could, within the context of a preliminary ruling, review the legality of a Council regulation in the light of international agreements concluded by the Council according to articles 228 and 238 of the EEC Treaty. The provisions of the agreement made an integrated part of the Community legal order.

20. *Molkerei Westfalen Case,* R.XIV:226:

"... que la Communauté constitue un nouvel ordre juridique, au profit duquel les États ont limité, bien que dans des domaines restreints, leurs droits souverains, et dont les sujets sont, non seulement les États membres, mais également leurs ressortissants".

21. *Salgoil Case,* R.XIV:675:

"... les dispositions des articles 31 et 32, alinéa, 1, ont pénétré dans l'ordre juridique interne et s'y trouvent directement applicable".

22. *Wilhelm Case,* R.XV:15:

"... les conflits la règle communautaire et les règles nationales en matière d'entente doivent etre resolus par l'application du principe de la primauté de la règle communautaire".

23. See for example the judgements of the Belgian Cour de Cassation May 27, 1971 in the case of *État belge v. S.A. Fromagerie Franco-Suiss Le Ski,* Journal des Tribunaux 1971, p. 471, and of Cour d'Appel de Paris July 7, 1973 in the case of *Director-General of Customs v. Société des Cafés and others,* Gazette du Palais, nos. 262—263, 1973. Note also the case from the Italian Court of Appeal, *Schiavello versus Nexi,* referred in *Giurisprudenza Italiana 1972,* I, pp. 1861—1868, in which the primacy of community law over subsequent Italian law was recognised.

24. See judgement by the German Federal Constitutional Court referred in NJW 1974, pp. 1697—1704, in the case of *Internationale Handelsgesellschaft mbH v. Einfuhr- und Vorratstelle für Getreide und Futtermittel.*

25. The position of directives differs from that of regulations, since they are only binding upon the states to which they are addressed but are also to be directly applied when comprising sufficiently detailed rules to directly create rights and obligations between the addressee and its individuals, see e.g. *Grand Case*, R.XVI:840, *Spa SACE Case*, R.XVI:1224 and *Van Duyn Case*, R.1974:1349:
"il convient d'examiner, dans chaque cas, si la nature, l'économie et les termes de la disposition en cause sont susceptible de produire des effets directs dans les relations entre les États membres et les particuliers".

26. See U Scheuner in *CMLReview 1975*, pp. 171—191, on Fundamental rights in European Community Law and in national constitutional law.

27. Note the excited comments in the French press when judgement 22/70 (*Commission v. Council*) was delivered on March 31, 1972 (R.XVII:263); see comments by J-V Louis, *opus cited*, p. 489.

28. *CMLReview 1970*, p. 174.

29. See A D McNair in *BYIL 1957*, pp. 1—19, W Lorenz in *AJCL 1964*, p. 1 f, F A Mann in *BYIL 1958*, p. 33 f and Brownlie, *opus cited*, pp. 15—21.

30. See note 29.

31. R B Schlesinger in *Revue intern. de droit comparé 1963*, p. 514 f.

32. See note 29.

33. R B Schlesinger, *opus cited*, page 518, see also W Friedmann, *The changing structure of international law*, pp. 188—210.

34. Note the statement by the Advocate-General Roemer in the *Plaumann Case* (R.IX:241) that the reference to national systems only concerned "responsabilité administratif" and not general law on liability. Cf. Advocate-General Lagrange in the *Meroni Case*, R.VII:351f:
"En droit allemand, la spécialité du dommage n'est exigée ni en droit civil ni administratif".

Too much importance should not be put on the non-conformity of these opinions, since it often concerns views of definitions and terminology. Note also that most national systems draw analogies from the civil liability to the public.

35. Advocated by A Heldrich, *Die allgemeinen Rechtsgrundsätze der ausservertraglichen Schadenshaftung im Bereich der Europäischen Wirtschaftsgemeinschaft*, p. 19 f and 161 f.

36. W Lorenz, *opus cited*, p. 8, F Dumon in *Cahiers 1969*, p. 38, L Goffin, *Droit des Communauté Européennes*, p. 154, McNair in *BYIL 1957*, p. 17, R B Schlesinger, *opus cited*, p. 520, P Reuter, *Mélanges à Henri Rolin*, p. 273. The Advocate-General Roemer (*Plaumann Case*, R.IX:241f) said that common principles should be orientated from the basic ideas according to how state liability was understood in the different states; the Court was in that procedure relatively free but had to respect "un cadre commun" in all the legal systems of the Member-States. Also Advocate-General Gand rejected a mini-denominator and thought it was a work of comparison and creation for the Court (*Kampffmeyer Case*, R.XIII:352).

37. *Die allgemeine Rechtsgrundsätze in der Rechtssprechung des Europäischen Gerichtshofs*, p. 8.

38. See Advocate-General Roemer in the *Plaumann Case*, R.IX:242.

39. Beiträge zum ausländischen öffentlichen Recht und Völkerrecht, Volume 44. See

also *Series Études* published by the Commission, no 12, 1971, Les recours juridiction-nels contre les actes administratifs spécialement économiques dans le droit des États membres de la CEE, p. 19 f.

40. Note some statements of the authors in the doctrine: A Donner, *opus cited,* p. 10:
"The aim is always to arrive at a concrete solution which links up with the judicial views held in the six countries and sometimes to go beyond these to form a kind of synthesis".

W Lorenz *opus cited,* p. 10:
"No particular national law of the 'six' should claim any preference over the others unless it can offer a superior solution to a problem, one best offer to serve the aims of the Treaties".

P Reuter, *opus cited,* p. 273:
"il s'agit bien plus de rechercher l'esprit des droit nationaux, leur orientation et leur évolution".

P Pescatore in *ZaöRVR 1972,* p. 246:
". . . the Court may take into consideration every relevant legal factor, whatever its nature and its source. Thus, it has made extensive use of the general principles of law and of the idea of 'legal convergence' between the national laws of the Member-States, that is to say, the method of comparative law. It is in this spirit that it has been able, in particular, on points where the Treaties are silent, to lay down foundations of fundamental rights in the Community legal order".

U Scheuner, *opus cited,* p. 185:
"The comparative analysis cannot cling to particular details, but must follow the general trend of the evolution of legal prescriptions; it must lead to a result acceptable in all member States".

Advocate-General Roemer thought in the *Werhahn Case* (R.1973:1258) it was not to seek the accord by all legal systems of the Member-States nor a majority but
"on appelé l'étude *pondéré* de droit comparé"

in which it might be important to point out the most developed system.

41. *ZaöRVR, 1972,* p. 241, see also *L'ordre juridique des Communautés Européennes,* p. 171 f in which he enumerates the most outstanding principles which have primarily been drawn from inspiration of the internal laws: principe de la légalité, principe de la bonne foi, protection de la confiance légitime, respect de droit acquis, exigences d'une bonne administration de la justice, refus de déni de justice, principe général de responsabilité de la Communauté, principe de la sécurité juridique, égalité devant les charges publiques, règle "non bis in idem", règle "non venire contra factum proprium". In applying general principles this procedure is said to tend to reflection and to comparative studies, but
"Le Processus, il est vrai, est plus intuitif qu'explicite"

(page 173).

Confer on the ECSC Treaty *Chatillon Case,* R.XII:280:
". . . des principes général de droit applicable en matière . . ."

and *Simet Case,* R.XVII:197:
". . . principes fondamentaux de droit en matière d'intérets . . .".

42. The French delegation in *Union Internationale des Magistrats* wrote (*Cahiers 1969,* p. 42 (Dumon)):
". . . ce qui n'est pas susceptible d'etre accepté n'est pas commun".

Note, there are no dissenting votes in the judgements, and one cannot thus measure the accord within the Court itself.

43. See L Goffin in *Droit des Communautés Européennes,* p. 155:
"Il ne parait pas que le texte étudié renvoie aux principes généraux de droit international public encore que les Communautés puissent encourir une responsabilité internationale".

P Pescatore in *CMLReview* 1970, p. 169 f, considers international law to be unsuitable for solutions of community problems.

44. See P Pescatore, *L'ordre juridique des Communautée Européennes,* pp. 172—173, U Scheuner, *opus cited,* p. 184 and A Donner, *opus cited,* p. 10.

45. See the Accession Treaty and Act concerning the conditions of accession and the adjustments to the treaties, articles 1—9, 29—30, and in particular article 2:
"From the date of accession the provision of the original treaties and the acts adopted by the institutions of the Communities shall be binding on the new Member-States and shall apply in these states under the conditions laid down in those treaties and in this act."

Although nothing is specifically and expressly stated as to the case-law of the Court one may as well comprehend that it is implicitly incorporated and accepted.

See further P Pescatore, *L'ordre juridique des Communautés Européennes,* p. 34 f.

46. See *Hauptzollamt Bremerhaven v. Massey-Fergerson,* R.1973:907.

Part Three
The Contractual Liability
of the Communities

Chapter ten

The Jurisdictions

§ 10.1 General positions

It was not necessary earlier to look closer at the border between non-contractual and contractual liability from a completely theoretical viewpoint, and by reasons practical in nature it was furthermore proper to proceed firstly with the examination of the non-contractual liability, since the Court has elaborated a case-law on that subject which may give guidance to the contractual liability on which there is no real case-law. However, it seems appropriate to pay a little more attention to the actual kind of liability, since it appears to have a certain significance with regard to various jurisdictions.

In article 178 of the EEC Treaty the Court is given the jurisdiction to compensate for damage provided for in article 215 (2) i.e. damages resulting from non-contractual liability; on this matter the Court has exclusive competency following from a comparison with article 183[1]. As to the contractual liability the Court will only be able to consider such liability seised with a dispute by the application of article 181. When that article is not applicable some other jurisdiction is competent which follows from comparison with article 183.

Article 215 (1) then is not intended to be applied exclusively by the Court like article 215 (2) but also by national courts and tribunals. Graphically, the various jurisdictions within the Communities will appear as follows (references are made to articles in the EEC Treaty):

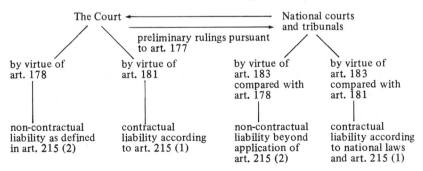

The borderline with regard to jurisdiction is in article 215 accordingly based on the notions of contractual and non-contractual liability of which the Treaty is devoid of fixed definitions. However, the Court has by virtue of article 178 ultimately the power to give application to article 215 (2) and by that to determine the scope and meaning of the non-contractual liability, which also implies drawing the line towards contractual liability, where the Court is bound by the limits resulting from the reference to general principles common to the laws of the Member-States.

The reason for the different systems available is of course based on the fact that the non-contractual liability covers the major part of the activities of the Community in carrying out the Treaty which cannot be subject to different views by various national authorities. When a national court or tribunal has doubt as to its competence in this respect the situation can be clarified by a reference to the Court for a preliminary ruling[2].

The competence of the Communities to conclude contracts emerges *inter alia* from articles 211 EEC, 185 EAEC and 6 ECSC Treaties. The capacity of an individual to conclude contracts will probably follow his personal law (domestic law).

§ 10.2 Suits before the Court

The case-law pertaining to article 42 of the ECSC Treaty concerns employment contracts of the community civil servants (that Treaty is devoid of an article corresponding to article 179 EEC Treaty) from the nineteen fifties and for the Rome Treaties there is no case-law at all so far on the articles giving competency to the Court on contractual matters. Article 42 in the ECSC Treaty was also brought into the discussion in the context of the competency of the Court under the Rome Treaties on employment contracts related to a period when no staff regulation had been adopted by the competent institutions. These cases also reveal some items on the applicable law which will be dealt with in the next chapter.

Article 181 EEC Treaty contains four main criteria 1) any arbitration clause 2) contained in a contract 3) concluded by or on behalf of the Community and 4) the applicable law may be private or public and does not affect the jurisdiction as such. An *arbitration clause* as the English version reads of the Treaties or in the French version a *clause compromissoire* seems to be unclear in meaning and importance; it has thus been said[3] that the parties do not submit their dispute to arbitration but to settlement following normal strict legal principles. Furthermore, in article 20 of the EAEC Treaty the parties may

"conclure un compromis à l'effet de saisir le comité d'arbitrage"

(conclude a special agreement in order to refer the matter to the Arbitration Committee); the decision from the Committee can be reviewed by the Court (article 18 (2)) as to its formal validity and to the interpretation of the Treaty made by the Committee. The notion *clause compromissoire* is adopted from the French legal system as well as "conclure un compromis etc." and the difference between these two notions in French law is[4], that the former is "un accord des parties, antérieur à tout différand, de soumettre à des arbitres celui entre elles"

but the latter "suppose le litige né" which fits the situation described in article 20 of the EAEC Treaty. The clauses furthermore bar an action before a civil court but a party has a certain possibility of appeal to a court of the arbitrators' award. The arbitrators have to follow normal rules of procedure and substantive law (article 1019 of *Code de procedure civile*); but the parties may also according to that article derogate from this rule in making the arbitrators *amiables compositeurs* with power to disregard normally applicable rules of law, with the exception of imperative rules and public policy, and also waive the right to appeal[5].

However, there can be no doubt concerning the effect of the *clause compromissoire* mentioned in the Treaties in ousting the jurisdictions of the national courts of the Member-States and then serving as a prorogation of jurisdiction in favour of the Court, but the question is whether the meaning attached to the French notion will have any impact on the parties' possibilities to suspend the rules of procedure of the Court and any effect on the applicable law. Concerning the procedural rules it emerges from the case-law where article 42 of the ECSC Treaty has been applied that those rules have not been affected, that is to say the normal procedure has been applied. As to the law applicable in those affairs, see § 11.3.1.

In the case of *Kergall* (R.II:35) the Court accepted competency in force of article 42 by an indirect reference to a prorogation clause i.e. the employment-contract contained a reference making the staff regulation applicable, when not contrary to the individual contract, and which contained a prorogation clause reading:

"Après épuisement des voies de recours administratives propres à chaque institution, les litiges auxquels pourra donner lieu l'application du présent règlement seront portés devant la Cour de Justice".

The Court took the same view in the cases of *Mirrosevich* (R.II:383) and *Bourgaux* (R.II:435) in which it added that the general terms of article 42 did not permit to conclude an obligatory limitation of a *clause compromissoire* which would in particular exclude the remedy of annulment. Note, however, that the Advocate-General thought the Court had competency by virtue of both article 42 and article 43 (1) in conjunction, since in his opinion the concerned *Statut du Personnel* constituted an additional provision of the Treaty (article 43 has no correspondence in the Rome Treaties). The competency of the Court in this respect has not been questioned since those cases. How far it is possible to remove from the plain wording of article 181 EEC in the sense that the *clause compromissoire* shall be contained factually in the contract, is however, difficult to tell but the inclusion is not indispensable according to French law, the parties' agreement to this effect may emerge through other means.

Furthermore, the wording of the articles may in itself imply that the clause should have been included or expressed in some way *before* the dispute arose, and since a *clause compromissoire* in French law implies in itself a stipulation in advance to any dispute and this taken together with the absence of a stipulation concerning the conclusion of a "compromis" one might understand by these indications that the Court should not agree to the parties' conferring jurisdiction *after* a dispute has arisen. Note also the *Convention on Jurisdiction and Enforcement of Civil and Commercial Judgements* (see further § 10.3) articles 12 and 15 prohibiting derogations from a certain jurisdiction posterior to the beginning of a dispute, but, nevertheless, such an interpretation seems to be in this context to narrow, since there appears to be no reasons from a substantial view-point (including legal protection of the weaker party) why the Court should not accept jurisdiction when asked by the parties to solve their dispute.

In the case of *Lachmüller* (R.VI:937) there was some uncertainty as to whether article 179 EEC Treaty was applicable or not, since according to that article the Court is competent to rule upon disputes between the Community and its servants on the conditions and to the extent provided for in a staff regulation or other relevant provisions but no such provisions had been adopted at that time. Since no reference had been made to the Court in the individual contracts by virtue of article 181 the national courts had been competent; however, the Court considered itself to have jurisdiction based on article 179, this was reinforced by the general provision in article 173 concerning its function of reviewing the legality of the acts of the Council and the Commission, which is a position which was maintained in similar subsequent cases.

A short summary shall be given concerning the Communities' practice in concluding contracts. The Commission has adopted rules of general terms and conditions governing supply contracts (*document 10070/IX/69*) involving nineteen articles regulating most matters arising out of those contracts. In article 16 it is established (English version) that the parties

"shall have recourse to arbitration before any legal actions are taken";

in the French version the parties

"font effectuer une expertise préalablement à toute instance judiciaire"

which more accurately describes the actual procedure. In the event that the parties cannot agree upon the assignement of an expert, he shall be appointed by the President of the Court. The expert shall within one month submit to the parties a report analysing the nature as well as the cause of the dispute and *propose* a complete and objective solution according to law and equity. When this procedure fails to produce an amicable settlement of the dispute, each party may submit the dispute to the Court to the exclusion of any other court (art. 17). Both parties must thus consent to the settlement suggested by the expert and there is thus no award of arbitration to be reviewed by the Court.

Local contracts of supply of gaz, electricity, water etc. are subjected to the local courts and domestic law which is the normal pattern of international organisations in this respect[6] unless peculiar needs of those bodies provoke special arrangements.

Concerning the Atomic Supply Agency contracts concluded by the Agency with persons domiciled within the Community's territory always contain a prorogation clause endowing the Court with exclusive competency in any dispute arising from the contract including also disputes pertaining to the question of the validity of the contract.

Concerning aid granted by the European Development Fund in the context of the *Yaoundé Convention* it is provided for in article 64 of the *Financing Regulation of the Council (71/68 EEC)* relating to the financing and administering of community aid that the Commission shall incorporate in the financial agreements concluded between it and a convention-state that

"... les litiges qui surviendraient entre la Communauté économique éuropéenne ou la Banque (the European Investment Bank), d'une part, et les bénéficiaires de toutes aides accordées sur les ressources du Fond, d'autre part, et qui seraient relatifs à l'interprétation ou à la mise en application desdites conventions de financement seront tranchés par la Cour de justice des Communautés européennes"

while the applicable law is left to the parties to indicate.

When the High Authority has granted loans to enterprises in the Member-States, jurisdiction has been conferred upon the Court[7] together with a choice-of-law clause referring to the law of the debtor[8]. The Court shall also have competency[9] on bonds floated by the High Authority in 1957 in the USA.

§ 10.3 Suits before national courts and tribunals of the Member-States

When the Court is not competent by virtue of a prorogation clause the national courts of the Member-States have general competency. National courts of non-Member-States are excluded from being automatically competent which appears from the wording of article 40 (3) ECSC Treaty

"... *les* tribunaux nationaux"

and Rome Treaties (artt. 183 EEC and 155 EAEC)

"*des* juridictions nationales".

Note the different wording of these articles in the ECSC Treaty and the Rome Treaties which, however, do not seem to imply any differences in substance. The Communities will accordingly not enjoy immunity from such suits before the national courts although the execution of a judgement rendered by a national court must be submitted to the Court in order to enable access to the assets of the Communities. Concerning the European Investment Bank one notes that body has been put into the shoes of any legal person in court proceedings before national courts and is also directly liable to execution by force of national judgements (article 29 of the Statutes of the Bank).

As to the competency of various national courts this matter is regulated by the Convention on Jurisdiction and Enforcement of Civil and Commercial Judgements[10] signed in Brussels 1968 as a result of article 220 of the EEC Treaty in which the Court was given the power by a special protocol signed in 1971 and came into force February 1, 1973 to give preliminary rulings concerning the interpretation of the Convention on similar terms as those established in article 177 of the EEC Treaty[11]. The basic principle is that a person is subject to the courts in the contracting state in which he is domiciled regardless of his nationality, i.e. the competence emerges from the domicile of the defendant; non-nationals follow the rules of nationals (art. 2). The convention does not contain any definition of domicile but leaves it to the judge to use concepts of his own national law in order to determine whether a party is domiciled in the country where the court is situated or not; in the negative case the judge may apply the law of another contracting state in order to determine if a domicile can be found in that country. If the defendant is not domiciled in a contracting state, the state concerned may apply its own otherwise applicable law, save as provided for in article 16. The seat of companies and other judicial persons will serve as a domicile in the application of the Convention (art. 53). A defendant domiciled in a contracting state may be sued before courts in a country other than where he is domiciled in special cases e.g. on contractual matters, delictual or quasi-delictual matters (artt. 5 and 6). Furthermore, exclusive competency has been granted regardless of domicile, e.g. on matters of real estate, dissolution of companies, registration of patents (art. 16). In article 17 the right is given to the parties to agree upon a prorogation clause but with certain limitations (artt. 12, 15 and 16). Litispendence and connexity are regulated in articles 21, 22 and 23. The convention together with the Treaties thus form from a structural view a complete and harmonious order concerning the competency of various jurisdictions within the Communities with the Court as sole and final coordinator[12].

There are a number of cases in which the High Authority has been a party before national courts both as plaintiff and defendant although not on contractual matters of which one notes *inter alia* nine cases from Italy mainly concerning the execution of judgements by the Court and decisions by the High Authority and thus involving interpretation of article 92 of the ECSC Treaty. Note also that an action before the Tribunal de première instance de Bruxelles, April 15, 1966 (*Vanhove versus High Authority*) concerned the recruitment of civil servants to which a community staff regulation was applicable upon which the Court was found to have exclusive competency to rule.

Concerning the law applicable to a contract between a Community and an individual, should such a case be brought before a national court, one may presume that the court will follow its own choice-of-law rules but cannot of course disregard relevant community legislation such as article 215 (1) EEC Treaty providing for the contractual liability to follow the law of the contract which implies the prevention of a fragmentation of the contract to several laws.

§ 10.4 Suits before national courts of non-Member-States

The Communities are international organisations and would from that fact generally enjoy immunity from suits and have their assets executed but an actual dispute between an individual and a Community brought before a national court of a non-member country would vary considerably depending on the issue and the law of that state in considering whether the law of that state favoured an absolute immunity or the doctrine of relative immunity. In the latter case the outcome would depend on whether the issue could be characterised as an act *juri imperii* or *juri gestions*; the doctrine of relative immunity seems, however, to gain force in application at least in Western Europe. Although immunity from proceedings may have been waived that does not always mean that immunity will be waived in execution of the judgement given concerning assets in that country. If, therefore, the situation is unclear in this matter, unless a complete submission has been expressly made by the Community as was done concerning the loan issued in Switzerland in 1956 by the High Authority in submitting itself to the jurisdiction of the ordinary courts of the Canton of Zürich of any dispute arising out of or in connection with the loan[13], it is certain that any judgement foreign to the Communities must be submitted to the Court for authorisation in order to be enforceable within the Community as well as any judgement rendered by the national courts of the Member-States.

If a clause conferring jurisdiction upon the Court in a contract between a Community and a party from a third country is to be respected by a court in such a country, this depends on the law of that country. Concerning the enforcement of a judgement rendered by the Court in a third country such a judgement will probably be considered in the same way as any foreign court decision and be subject to the normal rules applicable in such a situation in that country.

As to the practice of community organs one notes furthermore concerning the Atomic Supply Agency that contracts concluded with the US Atomic Energy Commission[14] are subject to US jurisdiction and will follow concerning the applicable law the Master Cooperation Agreement between the EAEC and the Commission and US national legislation. Contracts concluded with the USSR state trade agency contain an arbitration clause referring to the ICC rules of arbitration where the arbitrators are to sit in Stockholm or Zürich.

Footnotes chapter ten

1. The same applies to the EAEC Treaty; relevant articles are 151, 188 (2) and 155. Concerning the ECSC Treaty the construction is different inasmuch as the liability is provided for in articles 34 and 40; competency of national courts is given in article 40 (3); there are no specific provisions relating to the contractual liability but the Court will be competent when prorogated by the parties to a contract.

2. Cf. § 4.2.

3. See Stein and Hay in *AJCL 1960*, p. 406 and E H Wall, *The Court of Justice of the European Communities*, p. 153 f.

4. J Robert, *Arbitrage civil et commercial*, p. 96.

5. Confer the English system where the arbitrators are presumed to follow the law; note Arbitration Act 1950, article 20 according to which a question of law may be submitted to the High Court. Cf. also ICC's arbitration rules, article 19 (3).

6. C W Jenks, *opus cited*, p. 162 f.

7. G R Delaume in *AJCL 1957*, p. 193, note 13.

8. U Drobnig in *AJCL 1967*, p. 212, note 38.

9. G R Delaume, *opus cited*, p. 208.

10. For a commentary see *Bulletin of the EC*, Supplement 12/72.

11. See T Cathala in *Recueil Dalloz 1972*, pp. 24—31, and M R Mok in *CMLReview 1971*, p. 485 f.

12. Note, the Convention and the Protocol have not yet become applicable to the three new Member-States, but are subject to adaptation in the enlarged Community.

13. G R Delaume, *opus cited*, p. 209.

14. Note that USAEC in 1975 has been replaced by Energy Research and Development Administration (ERDA) and Nuclear Regulatory Commission (NRD).

Chapter eleven

Law applicable in proceedings before the Court

No case has yet been brought before the Court on contractual liability with the exception of such cases involving civil servants of the Communities. Nevertheless the whole bulk of community law gives some indications from which one could extract some general lines as to feasible directions the Court may follow in seeking solutions for judging cases of contractual liability. This implies taking a position on a range of questions *inter alia* pertaining to choice-of-law rules but also having due regard to community peculiarities and objectives. Consequently it seems impossible and pointless to try and give an exhaustive description of the Court's behaviour in all such instances which may arise in connection with those items where predictions will accordingly loose their preciseness the more details one enters into. Thus the aim of the following chapter will be merely to give a broad outline based on available indications and to reveal some of the main subjects involved.

§ 11.1 Introductory notes

For the Court to obtain the law applicable to a contract and thus also the law governing the contractual liability of the Community (art. 215 (1) EEC) this is a process which necessitates taking a position regarding choice-of-law rules in a broad sense. Two different situations are then discernible 1) a choice-of-law clause is incorporated or annexed to the contract or 2) the contract is devoid of any express stipulation to that effect. Such express choice-of-law clauses are found in contracts concluded by or on behalf of the Communities and are directly incorporated into *inter alia* the following contracts:

General public supply contract

"Save as may be otherwise stipulated in the special terms and conditions of contract, the law of the country in which the supplier has his registered office shall be applicable to the contract".

Subcontracts concluded by the Atomic Supply Agency with users in the Community under the Master Agreement with USAEC

"The contract shall be governed by the law applicable at the place where the contractor has his registered office",

to which it is sometimes added in certain contracts

"Toute interprétation du présent contrat devra etre conforme aux dispositions en vigueur du 'Master Agreement' et de l'Avenant. L'interprétation du 'Master Agreement' ne pourra se fonder que sur les dispositions qui y sont déclarées applicable dans le corps meme de ce document"[1].

The question is then whether the Court will accept these clauses or not. In order to answer this question, one solution is to obtain inspiration from the laws of the Member-States according to the procedure described in Chapter nine in the area of law relating to the parties' autonomy to designate the law applicable to their contract—common principles in the field of choice-of-law rules. However, the applicability of that procedure cannot be taken for granted, since concerning the non-contractual liability the Treaties of Rome expressly impose that procedure on the Court, which evidently implies certain limitations in the interpretation, but not concerning the contractual liability. Note however, such an approach was automatically adopted by the Court concerning the ECSC Treaty despite no reference to the laws of the Member-States with respect to both non-contractual liability and the Treaty as a whole which also goes for the Rome Treaties in general. This attitude is quite conceivable regarding the fact that the non-contractual liability affects almost all measures taken by a Community in its function as a public authority and is connected with the general interpretation of the Treaties, in which the Member-States have an important interest, and for which the Court has been created with exclusive competency to ensure the legal and proper performance. The contractual liability has a much more limited impact regarding the public authority function than the non-contractual, even though the contracts concluded serve the purpose of contributing to the functioning of the Communities but contain nevertheless important features of commercial law. One may therefore not exclude the possibility that the Court might feel more free in finding the law applicable to contracts[2].

In regarding the possibility of giving effect to the choice-of-law clauses quoted above one could imagine the Court considering whether the law of the other party to the Community of his residence, domicile, place of business etc. would follow such a stipulation, or whether the jurisdiction which otherwise would have been competent to rule the case would have accepted the clause, or some other way of procedure in handling those clauses. In this context one notes that the Court has had regard to national law for preliminary questions e.g. in the case of *Firma I, Nold KG versus the High Authority* (R.V:110f) in which the Court had to turn to German domestic law in order to determine the plaintiff's capacity in the court proceedings and representation as well as the validity of the application which had been signed by a lawyer under disciplinary measures as *Vertretungsverbot* where the Court had to interpret the law ruling the professional aspects of lawyers in Hessen. However, such procedures all seem to involve too many inconveniences which besides are increased when the other party to the Community is residing in a non Member-State; therefore one may perhaps expect that the Court might wish to adopt community rules which are more easily handled in dealing with those choice-of-law clauses to the benefit of legal security, predictability and procedural economics. Viewed in this context, it seems most natural that the Court also here should finally obtain inspiration from the national systems in creating such rules as to meet the needs of the parties' intentions expressed in a choice-of-law clause i.e. to recognise the party autonomy[3]. Since all national laws sustain that principle as such, no really serious problems seem to occur in adopting the parties' expressed intention, although one runs into certain differences in views considering theoretical frameworks, the extent and the exceptions to the rule. Furthermore, when a contract is devoid of a choice-of-law clause differences also appear which seem to be severe in their nature[4]. In the latter case the paramount question is what kind of choice-of-law rules the Court will create and if it is possible that such rules could result in applying substantive law of contracts created by the Court itself in accordance with the procedure described in Chapter nine.

§ 11.2 Party autonomy and the lex contractus

The autonomy of the parties can be considered as a general principle of the laws of the Member-States although there are peculiarities not to be neglected between one country and the other in its application, and it is useful to point out some of them in the context of some theoretical considerations ending with an appreciation of *lex contractus* to be formed by the Court.

In discussing theoretical views on the conflict of rules or laws, or private international law or choice-of-law rules it is necessary to keep in mind that when the national judge is seised with a case involving foreign elements i.e. elements rising the suspicion of the judge (or legislator) as to the appropriateness of considering a legal system other than merely his own, he is in fact dealing with rules of his own national legal system in considering whether or not he shall take account of those foreign elements and if so to what extent. There are thus no general rules giving guidance to judges all over the world on how to act in such instances but the exclusion of limited items covered by international conventions between a limited number of states, nor is there a coordinating body for the uniform interpretation by judges of various nationalities both in general and concerning the concluded international conventions. The starting point must then always be the national system and its courts both considered from a theoretical and practical viewpoint, since otherwise it is easy to run into misapprehensions and get lost in theoretical subtleties which often happens in the doctrine dealing with choice-of-law problems.

In principle it is important to make a distinction — even though the practical results may be the same — between a choice-of-law clause and when parts of laws in a foreign legal system in relation to *lex fori* by a reference have been incorporated into the contract itself, since these two kinds of clauses normally activate different sets of legal rules but only the former situation activates the authors of the doctrine. In the light of the considerations above it appears as misleading in this context to employ terms such as

"la compétence juridictionelle et la compétence législative",

for example, as did Yvon Loussourn in his article *Conflits de lois en matière de contrats dans le cadre CEE[5]*, but it appears conceivable in the light of the general traditional thinking prevailing in the doctrine. The notions of conflict rules and conflicts of law themselves seem improper and misleading to describe the realities involved, since it is not several national legal systems actually imposing themselves on the court seised with a case involving foreign elements, but it is the national judge according to his national concepts who tries to find a fairer solution to the case before him by additionally considering foreign legal systems than what his own domestic system alone can offer; thus there is no real conflict but a choice to make in order to arrive at the best possible solution of justice.

As to the actual situation in France concerning the parties' autonomy in contracts the French courts are rather liberal in accepting the expressed will of the parties concerning the law applicable when related to international trade. Theoretically the position is the objective localisation[6] that is to say one locates the contract according to various circumstances related to the contract of which the parties' intention is a capital element. The position in Belgium is close to the French. However, there are *inter alia* two striking consequences of that system 1) the parties' choice of law cannot differ from the localisation following from all circumstances relating to the contract and 2) the location will necessarily indicate a national legal system. In any event the French system provides the court with a workable tool in finding the proper law of a contract although with a certain inclination to the law of the place of performance, should an express choice-of-law clause be absent, this saves the court from running into dubious interpretations of an implied or assumed will of the parties as have the German courts when the contract is devoid of an express choice-of-law clause which otherwise would be followed to the point where there is no recognisable interest to uphold in the particular choice[7]. Devoid of an express clause by the parties the German courts devote much effort in finding the hypothetical will of the parties which is a procedure turning almost into an objective analysis of the contract in order to find the centre of its gravity. When this procedure fails one runs into a situation of important differences in comparison with the other national systems of the Communities, since the German courts try to find the proper place of performance of the various obligations resulting from the contract which is a procedure called *Spaltung* or *Zweirecht*; this means a split up of the contract and subjects it to several laws, which, however, to a limited extent may always happen but which one normally tries to avoid.

Concerning the Danish as well as the Dutch laws they accept party autonomy and are both favouring methods similar to the objective method should the contract be devoid of an express choice-of-law clause. The Italian courts have been bound by specific stipulations in *Code Civil* and *Code Commerce* in developing the autonomy of the parties but give effect to choice-of-law clauses. Not knowing the parties' intentions they apply *lex loci solutionis* or even the national law of the parties when coinciding.

According to Cheshire's interpretation of the position of English law[8] the parties have been able to choose the applicable law of their contract at least since 1796, which is done by an express clause to that effect or by prorogation to a judge in that country to solve the dispute. It is not necessary for the designated law to have any connection as such with the contract but should be *bona fide* and legal. When the expess choice is lacking the court will seek the presumed intention of the parties in which all facts and circumstances will be examined and standard presumptions may be overcome by elements in the particular case. However, the judicial basis of the proper law of the contract is divided into two schools, on the one hand, by Dicey and others advocating the subjective theory, and on the other, by Cheshire, Morris and others favouring the objective theory being close to the one advocated by Batiffol. Schmitthoff sees a reconciliation in combining the theories by first trying to find the law through the test of intention and if it fails by employing the objective theory[9].

Although the judge has found the law applicable to the contract in question it is not certain that he will apply all relevant rules of that law to his case but may omit to employ some of them because he may find them against the public order, which is related to his national concepts (*die Vorbehaltsklausul*), but foreign rules are also reprobated as belonging to foreign public law (criminal law, tax law etc.) or other foreign rules being contrary to public international law. The public order-mechanism has not in general been invoked by English courts as often as the mechanism has been on the continent which could probably be explained to a certain extent by the fact that English courts often apply *lex rei sitae* and *lex domicilii* on the one hand,

161

and, on the other hand, that for example French courts have accorded extensive liberty to the parties to choose *lex contractus* which has been neutralised by *ordre public*. A former rather extensive application of *die Vorbehaltsklausul* by the German courts had its main basis in article 30 of the EGBGB but according to Kegel the field of application is nowadays more limited[10].

The extent of application of *ordre public* evidently concerns the very basis for having choice-of-law rules at all, namely, speaking in general terms, one feels it is unfair to sentence an act considered legal in country A to be illegal in country B. From a practical viewpoint country B cannot hold all A's acts legal and fair, that is why it is sometimes necessary to have recourse to the institute of public order, but that does not mean that the judge in country B should resort to *ordre public* as soon as he dislikes a solution in country A in addition to cases in which the order in his country i.e. serious disturbance in his own legal system, is factually concerned[11]. In the field of matrimonial law strong feelings have been displayed in particular by the authors of the doctrine, but taking account in a case of the fact that for example a sheik may have twenty wives by the judge in a monogamous society does not mean he recommends bigamy to be introduced in his own country; fortunately the feelings have not been that strong concerning the law of contracts.

Furthermore, it is important in discussing the applicable law to note that, if, compulsory rules in *lex fori* are given up in favour of a foreign system such rules of that system may apply, or the matter in hand may be regulated in a different manner but one may nevertheless as a whole arrive at a similar result as if *lex fori* had been applied. Furthermore, as advocated by Sundström[12], the prorogation clause has the decisive importance on the effect of the actual outcome of a dispute, since the effect of the choice-of-law clause depends on many circumstances e.g. the actual circumstances of the material proofs, the rules in commercial law involve a great amount of discretion, the international trade follows its own rules and detaches itself from the national legal systems.

It is however important to consider the actual procedure when a national court approaches a case involving foreign elements with a view to a better understanding of the position of the Court. The most important step in a case involving foreign elements with respect to the outcome of the dispute is undoubtly what court will accept jurisdiction, since the influence of the legal thinking and concepts of *lex fori* on the interpretation of any applicable law can never be disregarded. This influence may of course vary according to courts and countries, and accordingly, if the parties have selected English law and wish that law to be applied as it is done in England they should of course choose a court situated in England and not one in any other country. This does not mean that such a court neglects the intentions of the parties regarding compliance with the applicable law but from actual circumstances it follows that one cannot have a court situated in country A applying the law of contracts of country B as it would have been applied by courts in that latter country, and there are several reasons for that:

   ... the specific legal thinking and concepts of *lex fori*

   ... commercial law involves a great amount of discretion on which the general legal thinking of *lex fori* is decisive

   ... procedural rules of *lex fori* do always apply

   ... foreign public laws do not normally apply

   ... the public order-mechanism.

Thus there are five main limitations on the effect of the choice-of-law clause which appears then as merely one element amongst many being determinant on the actual outcome of a dispute. Consequently it is not without reason that Sundström[13] speaks of the *correcting element* (*lex fori* is modified by foreign rules) and that the main problem is not the choice of a foreign legal system as such (normally a limited number to consider) but the finding of a workable formula with a view to adapting cases involving foreign elements into the needs of the international society.

The actual approach by a court seised with a case involving foreign elements is primarily, when once accepting jurisdiction which involves checking the case with regard to its substance in order to find out its competency according to jurisdictional rules as well as to general policies, to choose the law applicable to the contract which is quite easy when the parties have inserted a choice-of-law clause in their contract, otherwise the court will use other choice-of-law rules to find a proper law. The next step is to consider in what respect a chosen law differs in relevant parts from *lex fori* and correct the latter according to the foreign law on the differing points but with the reservations made above concerning the effects of the foreign law. Sometimes the rules and their motives are the same in both *lex fori* and the foreign law and no corrections are necessary from the view of the court. As to the qualification matter, the procedure described implies a rather practical approach, since the court has a set of actual circumstances which it relates to the chosen foreign law in order to find out the views which differ from *lex fori* and also tries to estimate a possible outcome under foreign law which makes the labelling of various branches of law a matter of minor interest[14].

When *les contractus* is viewed as above i.e. with *lex fori* omnipresent but corrected by elements from a foreign law found by the parties' intentions or otherwise, the question of the parties' liberty to choose the applicable law when diviating from the center of gravity or not, or lacking any obvious connection with the contract or whether the choice will entail frauds or evasive behaviours of the parties becomes far less exciting then normally presumed. Furthermore one should note that the concern of evasion is mainly related to *lex fori* and that the court seised with a case hardly ever considers whether a foreign law has been evaded, unless it is opportune from

163

the viewpoint of *lex fori*.

The views put forward concerning the national courts seem mainly to be relevant to the Court where the following situation appears:

... the main task of the Court is to ensure the legality of the integration process and it has in that context stated it ensures the respect of general principles of law of which the adherence to fundamental rights makes an integrated part. There is no reason to believe that basic rules on contracts arrived at by the formula envisaged in Chapter nine should not be embodied in the bulk of those general principles forming a part of community law (*lex fori*); here one notes in particular the notion of *contrat administratif* developed by the French *Conseil d'État* as well as by courts in Belgium and Italy, in which the administration is conferred certain unilateral powers of control in the public interest. In the common law system *government contracts* have been developed which are similar in nature to the civil law concepts. Furthermore, note community law contains legislation on contracts, e.g. general rules for the institutions in concluding contracts for the supply of goods and services, and hire contracts, general conditions for public work contracts and supply contracts financed by the European development fund;

... although the community law has no general expressed law on contracts, general principles of law will *inter alia* form standards which cannot be evaded or abused; but it is doubtful whether the Court will consider any national law as being evaded;

... community law and purposes (including general principles of law) can never be allowed to be contravened by any designated law applicable to a contract, which here constitutes the *ordre public*-mechanism in the community sense. Note in this connection the interpretation of *public policy* in article 48 (3) EEC in the *Duyn Case* (R.1974: 1337), and *force majeure* in the context of agricultural regulations in the *Internationale Handelsgesellschaft Case* (R.XVI:1139);

... there is no impact from a single national system regarding substantial law of contracts although the procedural rules of the Court will naturally apply but only one or two judges are more familiar with a designated law of the Member-States but that law will also be interpreted and appreciated by the judges of other nationalities.

The significance of those factors concerning the outcome of an actual dispute before the Court is difficult to estimate exactly, but they enable nevertheless to ascertain that the solution of an individual case will not be based on narrow concepts of a national law whatever law has been designated but will show features of an internationalisation; the law selected by the parties will provide elements of corrections to general concepts of contractual law and community rules in general. In this climate one may assume that the Court will accept references to laws other than the most obvious one connected with the contract which a national court might not do. If for example a contract is concluded between the Commission and a German company designating French law and being without obvious connection to that law, it is hard to see how the parties could become demoralised by the French law — at least from the view of the French judge in the Court; as a general rule, it appears, that the Court would accept any designated law of the Member-States, ever more so, since the Hague Convention on the law applicable to international sales, signed in 1955 and ratified *inter alia* by

Denmark, Belgium, France and Italy, stipulates in article 2

"la vente est régie par la loi interne du pays désigné par les parties contractantes"

when the sale is *international to its character* (the same concept is employed in the Preliminary Draft Convention, art. 1) which is a term not explained in the Convention other than in sofar that article 1, third paragraph, stipulates that a choice-of-law clause or a prorogation clause in a contract does not suffice to make the contract international; one or two more foreign elements should consequently be involved[15]. The Convention does not regulate the situation when a public international body is a contracting party to a contract; furthermore national courts normally have no jurisdiction over such bodies, but it seems that a contract as such can hardly ever become more international than when one party is a public international body. According to the aforementioned Convention the national judges can only consider a law related to a factual country which judges of normal civil courts also do in the Member-States which have not ratified the Convention. Moreover, the question of how the Court would react in the event the parties refer to public international law or general principles of law recognised by civilised nations seems in the light of the position outlined above not to raise any doubt as to their acceptance by the Court[16].

Finally, the question of *renvoi* (*Rück-* and *Wiederweisung*) shall be considered. Concerning the application of that notion in the context of contracts Germany seems to be the only Member-State employing that technic[17] where the Court can neither find an expressed nor implied intention of the parties. However, there seems to be no justification at all of *renvoi*, since once a country has laid down its own proper policy with regard to various choice-of-law rules, it is hard to understand why a court should use foreign rules to that effect in order to make a second choice concerning the law to be applied, and besides the notion involves a range of practical as well as theoretical inconveniences (e.g. the English doctrine of total *renvoi*), but the substantial reason for employing the technic is probably the inclination for arriving at *lex fori* in the final end. Furthermore one notes that the Convention on international sales excludes a *renvoi* in its second article, first paragraph, through the expression

"la loi interne du pays"

as well as Preliminary Draft Convention, art. 21. The application of the *renvoi*-technic in all its forms by the Court appears thus as being excluded in considering the positions of the national laws and the international character of the Court.

§ 11.3 The Absence of a choice-of-law clause

11.3.1 The cases of the civil servants of the Communities

As mentioned above there are some cases dating from the very beginning of the Communities respectively and directly touching upon the question of applicable law. First one notes four actions brought against the High Authority concerning employment contracts, and in all four cases the servants were submitted by a clause in their contracts to the Staff Regulation in force at that time unless the contract was contrary to the Regulation. In the *Kergall Case* (R.II:15) the Court stated that the contract disputed was a contract *sui generis* of the Community (page 22) and continued:

"Ce contrat doit etre interprété non seulement à la lumière des dispositions du Traité et du Règlement intérieur en vigueur auquel il se réfère, mais également en tenant compte de la volonté des parties et des intentions de la Communauté à l'égard de ses agent".

The Court furthermore concluded that the contract constituted a *contrat de droit public* having the advantage from the viewpoint of the servant of being submitted to administrative law in general and thus more rigid rules of law than civil ones and offering a better protection. Concerning the indemnity granted by the Court that was judicially based on article 40 and was accordingly non-contractual liability, since the Court found that the community administration concerned had exercised its public function in dealing with the contract which had not been done correctly (pages 21 and 25). In the cases of *Mirossevich* (R.II:371) and *Bourgaux* (R.II:370) the circumstances were similar.

In the *Algera Case* (R.III:89) the Court annulled decisions and granted indemnity; an essential question concerning the annulments was the revocation of illegal acts where the Court had recourse to general principles of the laws of the Member-States and also proceeded to make a comparative study to this effect (page 115). Concerning the indemnity granted the Court stated expressly (page 127) that the errors of the community administration were not contractual faults due to the fact that the plaintiffs had been allowed access to the Staff Regulation but that the basis of article 40 was the right one. The distinction between contractual and non-contractual liability seems here to be that any dealing under the Regulation in force, notwithstanding involving any contract, constituted an execution of the public function, being the crucial criteria, and thus made article 40 of the ECSC Treaty applicable.

Concerning the cases from the Rome Treaties one should note that the Court had competency by virtue of article 179 of the EEC Treaty also giving it *pleine juridiction* for the action for indemnity. In the case of *Lachmüller* (R.VI:937) the Advocate-General remarked upon the competency of the Court with regard to the action for indemnity (page 970) that article 178 granted the general competency and referred to article 215 (2) which dealt with non-contractual liability and article 215 (1) with contractual liability and drew the conclusion that the absence of a prorogation clause according to article 181 entailed that a reparation based on civil law was excluded but thought that

".. . en matière de litiges de personnel, la compétence de la Cour pour connaitre des recours en indemnités découle de facon générale de l'article 179".

Since article 179 states that the Court shall have jurisdiction

"in any dispute between the Community and its servants within the limits and conditions laid down in the Staff Regulation or Condition of Employment",

any dispute should embody the plaintiffs' actions. The Court had to find the law applicable to the contracts which according to article 215 (1) should also govern the action for liability. The Court did not exclude civil law in its considerations which emerges explicitly on page 953, and devoted furthermore half a page in order to determine the character of the contract which was considered as being public in its nature and from that concluded that it was submitted to *règles générales du droit administratif.* The main question was whether there existed a right to *stabilité d'emploi* and following the interpretation of the Treaty (i.a. art. 246 (3)), it emerged that there was no such right, but nevertheless this did not exclude a certain stability, and since the motives for the challenged decision were not sufficient with regard to the respect for the principle of *bonne foi* this omission constituted a contractual fault for which the Community was responsible. In the end of its judgements the Court referred to article 215 which was also done in the case of *Fiddelaar* (R.VI:1081) but the distinction was made in the case of *Leda de Bruyn* (R.VIII:45) in writing 215 (1).

In the case of *Fiddelaar* the situation was similar to the abovementioned case and the Court stated (page 1094) that general principles of administrative law applied, which were also to be applied in the case of *Leda de Bruyn* which appears indirectly on page 58 on the top. The Court stated that concerning the contract the decision of cancellation should at least be based on legally valid motives which was not the case.

11.3.2 Contracts in general
The description above confirms very well the aptness of the Court to create rules of law when necessary to solve disputes. If it is, on the one hand, very likely — not to say certain — that the Court will in general follow the parties' expressed intention in a choice-of-law clause although the exact effect of that clause is uncertain, it remains, on the other hand, to consider feasible steps by the Court when faced with a contract devoid of such an expressed intention and not related to the civil servants of the Communities, where *lex*

fori was applied. In those cases one must additionally take due account of the affairs as being internal matters of the Communities and also affecting labour including social considerations which would be absent in for example a purchase contract. However, one can say that the Court in these cases located the contracts according to the formula of the center of gravity relating to various connections.

Finally, concerning contracts in general it seems feasible that the Court may employ the procedure envisaged in Chapter nine to the situation when a contract is devoid of a choice-of-law clause. This would in general, it seems, with regard to the laws of the Member-State, entail seeking the center of gravity of the contract. Moreover, one may contemplate whether the Court would consider in this situation to interpret the prorogation clause also to involve a choice of *lex fori*, which would here entail a uniform law to be applied to contracts to which a Community is a party. One may hope the Court will not get into the temptation, although this approach may exceptionally be applied.

Footnotes chapter eleven

1. The Agency's responsibility according to the contract with the USAEC is imposed on the subcontractor who has to arrange the transport and take insurances. If for example the Agency's contract stipulate FOB USA harbour the subcontractor's liability will start at the FOB harbour.

2. U Drobnig thinks in *opus cited*, p. 213, that the Court should be free to adopt the most progressive methods in Europe in order to find the law applicable to contracts regardless of whether they emanate from the Member-States or not in the case a contract is devoid of a choice-of-law clause. Concerning such a clause it should be binding to the Court.

3. See *inter alia* L Goffin in *Droit des Communatués Européennes*, p. 169, Stein and Hay in *AJCL 1960*, p. 420 and W Lorenz in *AJCL 1964*, p. 6.

4. See J-D Bredin in *Journal du Droit International 1963*, pp. 938—963, Y Loussouarn in *Il diritto dell'Economia 1961*, pp. 783—801, H J Maier in *NJW 1962*, pp. 323—328, H Batiffol in *Les Problèmes juridiques et Économiques du Marché Commun*, pp. 74—82, A O Borum, *Lovkonflikter*, pp. 139—157, G C Cheshire, *Private International Law*, pp. 185—230, and R M Graveson, *Conflicts of laws*, p. 404 f.

5. *Opus cited*, p. 798.

6. J-D Bredin, *opus cited*, p. 937 and H Batiffol, *Droit International privé*, Volume II, p. 207 f. Note the cases from Cour the Cassation Civil of June 29, 1971, (cited by Y Loussouarn in *Revue Trimestrielle de Droit Commercial*, 1972, pp. 236—237) in which the court stated
"les juges du fond apprécient souverainement les circonstances qui déterminent la localisation d'un contrat d'où ils déduisent la loi qui lui est applicable".

7. G Kegel, *Internationales Privatrecht*, p. 235 f.

8. *Private International Law*, p. 192 f.

9. *The English conflict of laws*, pp. 105—117.

10. *Opus cited*, p. 167.

11. See the *Preliminary Draft Convention* on the law applicable to contractual and non-contractual obligations drafted under the auspices of the Commission, (doc. XIV/398/72/E), art. 22:
". . . manifestly incompatible with the public policy".

12. *TfR 1966*, p. 110 f.

13. *Three discussions on the conflict of laws*, p. 97 f.

14. However, the qualification problem cannot be neglected although the approach described simplifies the matter which may otherwise cause a rather complicated picture in particular in the field of personal and family law of which the former indeed may appear as a preliminary question in a dispute of a contract. Note that the *Hague Convention on international sales of corporeal chattels*, art. 5, excludes that matter from the law applicable to the contract as well as the Preliminary Draft Convention, art. 1.

The Rome Treaties have avoided questions of qualification matters in reading co.l-cerning the competency of the Court, any contract under private or public law and thus leaving it to the Court to determine the nature of the contract, which might have been labelled differently under the various laws of the Member-States. Furthermore, in this context it is very important to keep in mind that it is the court acting under *lex fori* which makes the qualification of the facts involved, and in this respect enjoys a rather huge amount of discretion in interpreting the foreign law and determining its extent of application, e.g. rules in foreign procedural law may be considered as substantial law or may not be applied because of being foreign procedural law. This operation may be employed in order to uphold an otherwise void contract, since one normally presumes that the parties have intended to conclude a valid contract, or in general, to achieve a fair result.

15. See P Kahn, *La vente commercial internationale*, p. 2 f, H Dölle in *Rabels Zeitschrift*, 1952, p. 167 f and B A Wortely in *Festschrift Lewald*, p. 410 f.

16. See C W Jenks, *opus cited*, pp. 150—155.

17. H Batiffol in *Les problème juridiques et economiques du Marché Commun* p. 77 f, G C Cheshire *opus cited*, p. 71 and A O Borum *opus cited*, p. 77 f and G Kegel, *opus cited*, p. 130.

Annex I
Summaries of cases

In the affair of *Kampffmeyer and others versus the Commission of the EEC*
(R.XIII:317) having the object of a demand for indemnity pursuant to article
215 (2) of the EEC Treaty, the plaintiffs were German importers of corn
who, in accordance with regulations no 19/62 and 31/63 for gradually establishing a common organisation of the market of corn, had on October 1,
1963, requested the German market-organisation for certificates of importations with a tax fixed at 0,00 DM which had been announced by the market
organisation the same day applying to the month of January 1964. The
market-organisation refused on October 3 to grant the requested import-
licences basing itself on a safeguard measure undertaken by the German
Government on October 1 pursuant to regulation 19/62, article 22 (1). In a
decision of October 3, 1963 the Commission authorised the German
Government to maintain the protective measure until October 4. However,
the Court declared this decision of the Commission to be illegal and annulled it in its judgement of July 1, 1965 (*Toepfer,* R.XI:526). Some of the
plaintiffs had accomplished their purchase-contracts concluded on October 1
and had paid the tax applicable, some had only demanded licences for
importations and other plaintiffs had annulled their contracts against
compensation payment; moreover, some of the plaintiffs had also demanded
the Commission to repair the damage caused by its decision. The Commission, however, contested any obligation of reparation.

The plaintiffs alleged that the Commission had committed a *faute de
service* in not suppressing the protective measure taken by the German
Republic but illegally maintaining it. They deduced from the *Vloeberghs
Case* that the mere violation of a legal rule intended to protect the injured
party was susceptible to justify an action for indemnity, which was said to be
sustained by the *Toepfer Case.*

The Commission interpreted the case-law of the Court concerning article
40 of the ECSC Treaty in such a way that an objectively illegal behaviour
was not in itself grounds for an action concerning responsibility but a subjective fault had to be included in this behaviour, which should be applied
here.

The Court established that the behaviour of the Commission constituted a
faute de service rendering the Community liable by its erroneous application of
article 22 of regulation no 19/62, since the circumstances did not justify
protective measures and, though knowing the demands for certificates of
importation, the Commission had caused damage to the importers who had

acted according to the information conveyed in accordance with the community legislation. The fault did not consist in an erroneous appreciation of the facts involved but in the whole behaviour which in particular was manifested by the abusive usage of article 22.

Concerning the damage, the Court had been informed by the plaintiffs that actions for indemnity had also been brought before German jurisdiction against the German Republic to incur its liability. Therefore, to avoid different appreciations of the same damage by different jurisdiction applying different rules of law which might result in an insufficient or exaggerated indemnity, the plaintiffs were to present these judgements to the Court and also written proofs that they had exhausted all administrative as well as judicial remedies in order to obtain reimboursement of the unduly paid tax. The Court also made pronouncements concerning the existence and evaluation of the damage.

Regarding the plaintiffs who had only requested for importation licences, their actions for indemnity were rejected, because their operations were merely in the stage of purporting to do business and to make a profit; this was not sufficiently concrete for carrying a right to reparation.

In the affair of *Lütticke GmbH versus the Commission of the EC* (R.XVII:325) the object of the action was indemnity according to article 215 (2) of the EEC Treaty. The plaintiff imported milk-products — especially milk powder — to the German Republic and alleged that the Republic had imposed a tax on milk powder of such a height that it was incompatible with the Treaty and particularly article 92 (1) thereof, and as a consequence of this he had paid during the years 1962, 1963 and 1964 a tax of 124.396,04 DM. The basis of the action was the omission by the Commission of not having issued a directive or a decision to the German Republic by virtue of article 97 (2) in order to suppress the tax counted from January 1, 1962 or at least to reduce the tax to a level compatible with the provisions in articles 95 and 97 (1).

The Court established that community responsibility presupposed that the following conditions were present: a real damage, the existence of a causal connection between the alleged prejudice and the behaviour of which the institutions are accused and the illegality of that behaviour. The Court proceeded to examine whether the Commission in its acting had failed in its duties in accordance with article 97 (2). Since the Court found that the Commission in this case had not omitted to exercise its mission of surveillance, and, besides, the plaintiff had not shown, concerning the product in question, that an average tax of 3 % exceeded the limits appearing in the articles 95 and 97, which the Commission was called to safeguard, the action was rejected.

In the case of *Aktien-Zuckerfabrik Schöppenstedt versus the Council* (R.XVII:975) the object of the action was payment of indemnity for damage caused by regulation 769/68 of the Council prescribing the necessary measures to compensate for the difference between the national prices of sugar and the community price applied as from July 1, 1968; the regulation authorised the Member-States to grant compensation on certain conditions when the national price was higher than the price applied; from that day a common organisation of the sugar-markets had been established by regulation no 1009/67 of the Council. The plaintiff produced brown sugar and alleged that the German price of brown sugar was visibly much higher than the price prevailing as from July 1, 1968 and the difference between these prices could not be ignored. The German Republic did not grant any compensation at all. The damage was estimated at 155.411,13 DM. The Council had committed a *faute de service* in adopting the regulation which violated certain provisions of community law having the character of *Schutznormen*.

The Court stated that

".. . qu'en l'espèse, la responsabilité extracontractuelle de la Communauté supposerait à tout le moins le caractère illicite de l'acte prétendument générateur du préjudice;

que, s'agissant d'un acte normatif qui implique des choix de politique économique, cette responsabilité de la Communauté pour le préjudice que des particuliers auraient subi par l'effet de cet acte ne saurait etre engagée, compte tenu des despositions de l'article 215, alinéa 2, du traité, qu'en présence d'une violation suffisamment caractérisée d'une règle supérieure de droit protégeant les particuliers; que, partant, l'examen de la Cour dans le présent litige doit, en premier lieu, porter sur l'existence d'une telle violation;. . ."

and, since the Court did not find the mentioned condition satisfied, the action was dismissed.

In the affair of *Compagnie d'approvisionnement, de transport et de crédit SA and Grands Moulins de Paris SA versus the Commission* (R.XVIII:391) the plaintiffs alleged that the Commission had by neglectful behaviour caused them damage which should be repaired.

The Council had adopted by virtue of article 103 of the EEC Treaty regulations concerning certain measures relating to the economic situation in the agricultural sector necessitated by the devaluation of the French franc in 1969. In regulations by the Commisson the amount of import subsidies had been determined*. The plaintiffs alleged they had suffered damage insofar as the amount of subsidies should have been fixed at a higher rate. The low rate was illegal and contrary to the Council's regulations, since a higher rate

---

*Compagnie d'approvisionnement had lodged an action of annulment concerning these provisions of a regulation which had been rejected by the Court as inadmissible, since it concerned a regulation which did not affect the plaintiff individually.

would have been obtained, if all relevant elements had been taken into account. The calculating of the rate of subsidies constituted *une negligence fautive*. Furthermore, the Commission had infringed article 40 of the Treaty. The plaintiffs took the view that concerning regulations, each illegality should be considered as a fault. The plaintiffs also thought that the Commission was responsible, even though there was no illegality, in basing themselves on the case-law of the French *Conseil d'État* which recognised public responsibility in cases of a *préjudice anormal et spécial*.

The Commission answered that, even if there was an illegality, it did not result from a fault but an excusable error in the interpretation. Concerning the argument that each illegality constituted a fault the Commission stressed that such a rule was neither a principle common to the laws of the Member-States nor had it any support in the case-law of the Court.

The Court found the contested regulations to be legal and accordingly there was no point in examining the other conditions relating to liability for illegal behaviour.

Concerning responsibility based on criteria other than illegality the Court stated in *attendu* 46 and 47, page 409:

"...qu'une responsabilité éventuelle du chef d'un acte normatif légal ne saurait etre envisagée dans une situation telle que celle de l'espèce, compte tenu du fait que les mesures prises par la Commission ne visaient, dans un intéret économique général, qu'à atténuer les conséquences résultant, notamment pour l'ensemble des importateurs francais, de la décision nationale de procéder à une dévaluation du franc; que, dès lors, le moyen n'est pas fondé";

accordingly, the actions were dismissed.

In the case of *R and V Haegeman Sprl versus the Commission* (R.XVIII: 1005) the plaintiff asked the Court to declare certain regulations imposing a tax on imported wine from Greece to be inapplicable in the territories of Belgium and Luxembourg, to annul the decision by the Commission in which the plaintiff had been refused the benefit of being exempted from the tax, order the restitution of the tax, and finally, to grant indemnity, independent of the annulment and the restitution to the plaintiff, in order to repair the exceptional damage caused to the plaintiff in terms of loss of profit, unforeseen expenditure and losses on current contracts. The Council had in regulation no 816/70 laid down supplementary rules relating to the organisation of the common market of wine which included the establishment of a compensatory tax on wine concerning which the Commission had in its regulations issued rules of the modalities as to the application of the tax where no distinction was made concerning the provenance of the wine subject to the tax.

The Court expressed that the disputed tax was a part of the Community's own resources which here were gathered by national authorities and by national means; the plaintiff should therefore refer himself to the national authorities who were competent to handle such a demand for obtaining reimboursement of the tax, and, if necessary, article 177 could be used in order to secure the uniform application of community legislation. Therefore, the refusal by the Commission was not susceptible to an action of annulment and the action was inadmissible.

Concerning the allegation by the plaintiff that the Commission by its behaviour had caused the plaintiff damage the Court took the view that the Community's liability was linked up with the legality of the gathering of the disputed tax and that the relationship between the individuals and tax-authorities belonged to national jurisdiction and therefore, for the time being, the action of indemnity was rejected.

In the case of *Wünsche Handelsgesellschaft versus the Commission* (R.1973: 791) the plaintiff alleged that the Commission had caused damage, which should be repaired, by its regulation no 1643/71 instituting a minimum price-system which was applicable to imported concentrated tomatoes coming from Greece. The regulation was said to be illegal (in particular article 2 thereof), and the Commission had incurred the liability of the Community in adopting it. The validity of the regulation had already been examined in an earlier case within the framework of a preliminary ruling by the Court, but the plaintiff wished to put forward further evidence; however, the Court did not find this strong enough to permit the establishment of a sufficiently characterised infringement of a superior rule of community law aimed at protecting individuals; consequently, the action was rejected.

In the case of *Merkur Aussenhandels-GmbH versus the Commission* (R.1973: 1055) the plaintiff alleged that the Commission had infringed regulation no 974/71 of the Council and article 40 of the EEC Treaty by its regulations no 1014 and 1687/71 which did not provide for export compensation for the period May 12 to August 2, 1971 of products based on barley arranged for in the Council regulation. The Commission had thereby committed a fault in not being sufficiently diligent and thereby also causing damage to the plaintiff estimated at 50.000 DM.

In the Commission's first regulation certain products had been enumerated together with the amount of compensation. However, the products which the plaintiff mainly exported were not included until regulation 1687/71 was issued some months later. The plaintiff had asked the competent national authority to grant him compensation which however had been refused and against which he appealed. Since the plaintiff had brought an action before the Court, that national authority was waiting for the Court's decision before finally deciding the plaintiff's action. The plaintiff also asked the Commission retroactively to incorporate the products concerned which it had refused.

The Commission claimed primarily that the action by the plaintiff was not well-founded and secondly referred the plaintiff to exhaust means before national authorities in order to obtain the amount of compensation.

The Court did not find the alleged regulations to be illegal and the action could therefore be dismissed without necessitating the examination of the other conditions pertaining to non-contractual liability pursuant to article 215(2).

In the case of *Werhahn and others versus the Council and the Commission* (R.1973:1229) the object of the actions was indemnity according to article 215(2) of the EEC Treaty, where the Council and the Commission were alleged to have caused damage during the cereal campaign 1971—72 to the plaintiffs by defective planning, irrational and illegal organisation, in particular concerning wheat. The effect on the German purchaser was that he had to buy wheat from third countries at the threshold price of 125,25 units of account whilst his French and Italian competitors could buy it at a price close to the intervention price of 112,44 units of account, i.e. the Germans were discriminated. As a further action the plaintiff had cited the existence of a principle according to which indemnity should be paid by a public authority as a consequence of an illegal intervention similar to an expropriation.

Since the Court did not find any of the regulations mentioned to be illegal the main action was dismissed. Concerning the subsidiary claim there was no reason to penetrate whether such a principle was embodied in article 215(2), since the incriminated interventions were not illegal.

In the case of *Holtz & Willemsen GmbH versus the Council and the Commission* (R.1974:675) the plaintiff who run and oil-mill, considered in the context of the organisation of a common market for oil-plants (applied from July 1, 1967), within which a certain aid was paid to oil-producers utilising grains of rape cultivated in the Community, that the supplementary aid granted to factories situated in Italy, which had been prolonged year by year by the Commission, consituted an infringement of the Treaty as being discriminatory as to nationality. This was an administrative fault by the authorities elaborating and adopting the concerned regulations. As a result of this fault the plaintiff had suffered damage for which indemnity was asked. Furthermore, the plaintiff had in an action pursuant to article 175 of the EEC Treaty tried to bring the Council to supplement the application of the extra aid also to apply to factories being in an identic situation to the Italian ones, as for example his own factory. The action was rejected as inadmissible, since it concerned a regulation not affecting the plaintiff directly and individually (R.1974:1).

The Court pronounced concerning the supplementary aid to Italy that it only could be justified by special circumstances relating to the concerned national market as a whole. In the process of establishing a common market in the concerned agricultural sector the Council could prescribe temporary measures in order to mitigate the difficulties of the Italian factories which otherwise to a great extent would have been cut out of the market; it had not been suggested that the German market would have encountered similar difficulties. However, there was a risk that such a measure would permanently exclude a country from the common organisation of the market, but considering the problem in hand, the Council had respected the provisional character of the measure when applying it to the campaign 1973/74 for the last time. Therefore, the action was not sufficiently judicially founded and also dismissed.

In the case of *Comptoir national technique agricole (CNTA) SA versus the Commission* (R.1975:533) the plaintiff claimed reparation for damage resulting from the abrogation by the Commission of granting compensation applicable to exportation of grains of rape and therefrom obtained oil.

In regulation 17/72 of December 31, 1971 the Commission had determined the compensation applicable to France to be 3,95 FF per 100 kg grains from January 3, 1972 onwards; regulation 144/72 of January 21, 1972 increased the amount to 4,75 FF from January 24, 1972. By regulation 189/72 of January 26, 1972 the Commission suppressed the compensation counted from February 1, 1972, since the compensation was considered not to be indespensible in order to avoid disturbance in the trade of the products concerned. The plaintiff had the view that nothing had interfered between regulations 144 and 189 that justified the suppression and estimated the damage caused to him to 976 375,74 FF through applying the compensation of 3,75 FF to quantities of grain which had been predetermined before February 1, 1972. The plaintiff alleged that regulation 189 violated the basic regulation 974/71 of the Council as well as the principle of legal security comprising the non-retroactiveness of laws and the protection of the legitimate confidence of the interested parties (*Vertrauenschutz*).

The Court neither consider regulation 189 to be illicit with regard to regulation 974/71, nor had regulation 189 retroactive effects in the proper meaning of that term. The Court pronounced that the payment of compensation should not be considered as a guarantee against the risk of changes of the rates of currences, but (considerations 41 and 42 on pages 548—549):

"qu'il n'en reste pas moins que l'application des montants compensatoires écarte en pratique le risque de change, de sorte qu'un opérateur, même prudent, peut être amené à ne pas se couvrir contre ce risque;

que, dans ces circonstances, l'opérateur peut légitimement avoir confiance que pour des opérations irrévocablement engagées par lui parce qu'il a obtenu, sous caution, des certificats d'exportation comportant préfixation du montant de la restitution, aucune modification imprévisible n'interviendra qui aurait pour effet, en lui reimposant le risque de change, de lui causer des pertes inévitables".

Though there was no decisive public interest to do so, the Commission had nevertheless suppressed, with immediate effect and without prior notice, the application of the concerned payments of compensation without any transitional measures. Through violating the legitimate confidence in community law in not including transitional measures to protect the merchants in regulation 189, the Commision had violated a superior rule of law, which incurred the Community's liability. The parties were ordered to submit to the Court the figures of the indemnity reached by common accord or their figures arrived at individually.

Annex II

Bibliography

Adam, H-T
  Les organismes internationaux spécialisés. Contribution à la théorie générale des établissements publics internationaux. Vol. I. Paris 1965. (Bibl. de droit intern. 29)
André, Achim
  Konkurrierende Ersatzansprüche vor deutschen Gerichten und dem Europäischen Gerichtshof. Neue Juristische Wochenschrift. 1968.
Arendt, Ernest
  Luxembourg. Haftung des Staates für rechtswidriges Verhalten seiner Organe. Länderberichte und Rechtsvergleichung. Internationales Kolloquium veranstaltet vom Max-Plank-Institut für ausländisches öffentliches Recht und Völkerrecht (Heidelberg 1964). Köln 1967.
Aubert, Francois
  La cour de justice des communautés européennes. Revue Trimestrielle de Droit Européen. 1966.
Baade, Hans
  "Constitution-making" treaties and international courts: judicial review within the EC. De lege pactorum. Essays in honour of Robert Renbert Wilson. Durham 1970.
Batiffol, Henri avec le concours de Paul Lagarde
  Droit international privé. Vol. II. 5 ed. Paris 1971.
Batiffol, Henri
  Les conflits de lois en matière de contrats dans la CEE. Les problèmes juridiques et économiques du Marché Commun. (Colloque des Facultés de Droit, Lille 1959.) Paris 1960.
Bépoit, Francis-Paul
  Le droit administratif francais. Paris 1968.
Biever, Tony
  Livre jubilaire du Conseil d'État 1856—1956. Luxembourg.
Blanchet, Jean
  La concurrence du recours en annulation avec l'action en réparation des dommages. 1. Co-rapport. Kölner Schriften zum Europarecht. Bd. I. Köln 1965.
Bogaert, E van
  La caractère juridique de la Cour de Justice des CE. Mélanges offerts à Henri Rolin ... Problèmes de droit des gens. Paris 1964.
Borum, A O in collaboration with A Philip
  Lovkonflikter. 8 ed. Copenhagen 1970.
Bredin, Jean-Denis
  Conflicts of laws in contract matters in the EEC. Journal de Droit International. 1963.

Brownlie, Ian
Principles of public international law. 2 ed. Oxford 1973.
Cambier, Cyr
Luxembourg. Haftung des Staates . . . Köln 1967. See further Arendt.
Cartou, Louis
La concurrence du recours en annulation avec l'action en réparation des dommages. — Rapport général. Kölner Schriften zum Europarecht. Bd. I. Köln 1965.
Cathala, Thierry
L'interprétation uniforme des conventions conclues entre États membres de la CEE en matière de droit privé. Recueil Dalloz. 1972.
Cheshire, G C
Private international law. 7 ed. London 1965.
Chevallier, Roger-Michel
Methods and reasoning of the European Court in its interpretation of community law. Common Market Law Review. 1964.
Constantinesco, Léontin
La spécificité du droit communautaire. Revue Triméstrielle de Droit Européen. 1966.
Delaume, Georges R
Jurisdiction of courts and international loans. A study of lenders' practice. American Journal of Comparative Law. 1957.
Delbez, Louis
Les principes généraux du droit international public. 3 ed. Paris 1964.
Donner, André M
National law and the case law of the Court of Justice of the EC. Common Market Law Review. 1963.
Drobnig, Ulrich
Conflict of laws and the European economic community. The American Journal of Comparative Law. 1967.
Dumon, Frédéric
La responsabilité extracontractuelle des CE et de leurs agents. Articles 40 CECA, 215 CEE et 188 CEEA. Resolutions de l'Union internationale des Magistrats. 6 session. 1967. Cahiers de Droit Européen. 1969.
Dölle, Hans
Die 7. Haagerkonferenz. Rabels Zeitschrift 1952.
Elster, Theodor
Non-contractual liability under two legal orders. Common Market Law Review. 1975.
Ferrière, Georges
Le controle de la légalité des actes étatiques par la Cour de Justice des CE. Paris 1968.
Forsthoff, Ernst
Lehrbuch des Verwaltungsrechts. Bd. 1. 9 neubearb. Aufl. München 1966.
Friedmann, Wolfgang
The changing structure of international law. London 1964.
Galeotti, Serio
Italie. Haftung des Staates . . . Köln 1967. See further Arendt.
Germer, Peter
De europaeiske faellesskabers erstatningspligt udenfor kontraktsforhold: Et praktisk anvendelseområde for den komparative retsforskning. Juristen. 1967.

Goffin, Léon
La responsabilité de la CECA du chef de fautes différentes de la faute de service. Journal des Tribunaux. 1963.
Responsabilité non contractuelle. Cahiers de Droit Européen. 1968.
Annotation. /Plaumann & Co contre Commission de la CEE. Affaire 25/62. Arret du 15 juillet 1963./ Common Market Law Review. 1963.
La responsabilité non contractuelle des Communautés. Droit des Communautés Européennes. Les Nouvelles. 1969.
Goffin, Léon et Mahieu, Michel
Règlements et responsabilité des états. Cahiers de Droit Européen. 1972.
Responsabilité extracontractuelle des Communautés. Cahiers de Droit Européen. 1972.
Grdic, Katarine et al.
The present institutional and administrative position in the EEC. Eurocooperation. 1973:3/4.
Green, N A Maryan
International law. Law of peace. London 1973.
Graveson, R M
Conflicts of laws. 7 ed. London 1974.
Griffith, J A G & Street, Harry
Principles of administrative law. 3 ed. London 1963.
Heldrich, Andreas
Die allgemeine Rechtsgrundsätze der ausservertraglischen Schadenshaftung im Bereich der Europäischen Wirtschaftsgemeinschaft. Frankfurt am Main 1961. (Arb. z. Rechtsvergleich. 10.)
Art. 215 II des EWG-Vertrages — ein Irrweg zu europäischer Rechtseinheit. Juristenzeitung. 1960.
Ipsen, Hans Peter
Kunkurrenz zwischen Amtshaftung der EWG and der Bundesrepublik: primäre Haftung der EWG-Kommission; Art. 215 EWGV, § 839 BGB, Art. 34 GG. Europarecht. 1969.
Jaenicke, Günther
Bundesrepublik Deutschland. Haftung des Staates . . . Köln 1967. See further Arendt.
Jenks, C Wilfred
The proper law of international organisations. London 1962.
Kahn, P
La vente commerciale internationale. Paris 1961. (Diss. Dijon.) (Bibl. de droit commercial. 4.)
Kegel, Gerhard
Internationales Privatrecht. Ein Studienbuch. 2 neubearb. Aufl. München 1964.
Knöpfle, Robert
Die Schadensersatzklage und ihr Verhältnis zur Nichtigkeitsklage. — 2. Korreferat. Kölner Schriften zum Europarecht. Bd. 1. Köln 1965.
Das Verhältnis der Amtshaftungsklage zur Nichtigkeitsklage im Montanvertrag. Neue Juristische Wochenschrift. 1961.
Korsch, Hans
Prozessmaximen. — 1. Korreferat. Kölner Schriften zum Europarecht. Bd. 1. Köln 1965.
Lagrange, Maurice
The non-contractual liability of the Community in the ECSC and the EEC. Com-

mon Market Law Review. 1965/66.

Lecheler, Helmut J
Die allgemeinen Rechtsgrundsätze in der Rechtsprechung des Europäischen Gerichtshofes. Erlangen-Nürnberg Diss. 1967.

Lecourt, Robert
Le juge devant le Marché Commun. Genève 1970. (L'Institute Universitaire des Haute Études Internationales.)

Lorenz, Werner
General principles of law: Their elaboration in the Court of Justice of the EC. American Journal of Comparative Law. 1964.

Louis, Jean-Victor
Compétence internationale et compétence interne des communautés. Cahiers de Droit Européen. 1971.

Loussouarn, Yvon
Les conflits de lois en matière de contrats dans le cadre de la CEE. Il diritte dell'Economia. 1961.
Droit international du commerce et Marché commun. Revue Triméstrielle de Droit Commercial. 1972.

Løddesøl, Leif Terje
Domstolen i det europeiske ökonomiske fellesskap — en juridisk nyskapning? Tidsskrift for Rettsvitenskap. 1963.

Maier, Hans Jakob
Internationales Privatrecht (Schuldenrecht) in Europa. Neue Juristische Wochenschrift. 1962.

Mann, F A
The proper law of contracts concluded by international persons. British Yearbook of international law. 1959.

McMahon, J F
The Court of the EC. Judicial interpretation and international organization. British Yearbook of international law. 1961.

McNair, A D
The general principles of law recognized by civilized nations. British Yearbook of international law. 1957. The law of treaties. Oxford 1961.

Mok, M R
The interpretation by the European Court of Justice of special conventions concluded between the Member States. Common Market Law Review. 1971.

Monaco, Riccardo
Les principes d'interprétation suivis par la Cour de Justice des CE. Mélanges offerts à Henri Rolin ... Problèmes de droit des gens. Paris 1964.

Much, Walter
Die Amtshaftung im Recht der Europäischen Gemeinschaft für Kohle und Stahl. Frankfurt am Main 1952.
Die Haftung der Europäischen Gemeinschaften für das rechtswidrige Verhalten ihrer Organe. Die Haftung des Staates ... Köln 1967. See further Arendt.

Nafilyan, Gérard
Affaire 70/69. Arret du 16.3.1971. FERAM S.p.A. contre Commission des CE. Articles 40 et 53 du Traité CECA. Mécanisme de péréquation de ferraille. Revue Triméstrielle de Droit Européen. 1972.

Noel, Emile
How the European Communities' institutions work. Brussels 1973. (Community topics. No 39.)

Odent, Raymond
  Contentieux administratif. Vol. IV. Paris 1970—71.
Papier, H J
  Zur Reform des Staatshaftungsrecht. Deutsches Verwaltungsblatt. 1974.
Perry, R H
  Charles Worth on negligence. 4 ed. London 1962. (Common Law Library. No 6.)
Pescatore, Pierre
  International law and community law — a comparative analysis. Common Market Law Review. 1970.
  Legal problems of an enlarged EC. London 1973.
  Objectifs de la communauté comme principes d'interprétation. Miscellanea W J Ganshof van der Meersch. Vol. 2. Bruxelles 1972.
  L'ordre juridique des Communautés Européennes. Liège 1973.
Pescatore, Pierre with collaboration of A M Donner, R Monaco & H Kutscher
  Aspects of the Court of Justice of the EC of interest from the point of view of international law. Zeitschrift für ausländisches öffentliches Recht und Völkerrecht. 1972.
Piret, René
  La responsabilité sans faute en droit comparé. Centre interuniversitaire de droit comparé. 5ième congrès de droit comparé à Bruxelles. 1958.
Prins, W F
  Niederlande. Haftung des Staates . . . Köln 1967. See further Arendt.
Reuter, Paul
  Le recours de la Cour de Justice des CE et des principles généraux de droit. Mélanges offerts à Henri Rolin . . . Problèmes de droit des gens. Paris 1964.
Rigaux, Francois
  Le pouvoir d'appréciation de la Cour de Justice de CE à l'égard des faits. Miscellanea W J Ganshof van der Meersch. Vol. 2. Bruxelles 1972.
Rivero, Jean
  Droit administratif. 3 ed. Paris 1965.
Robert, Jean
  Arbitrage civil et commercial. 3 ed. Paris 1961.
Schermers, Henry G
  Community law and international law. Common Market Law Review. 1975.
  The law as it stands on the appeal for damage. Legal issues of European integration. 1975/1.
Schlesinger, Rudolf B
  Fonds commun des systèmes juridiques. Observations sur un nouveau projet de recherche. Révue International de Droit Comparé. 1963.
Scheuner, Ulrich
  Fundamental rights in European community law and in national constitutional law. Common Market Law Review. 1975.
Schmitthoff, C M
  The English conflict of laws. 3 ed. London 1954.
Stein, Eric & Hay, Peter
  Legal remedies of enterprises. American Journal of Comparative Law. 1960.
Street, Harry
  Great Britain, Haftung des Staates . . . Köln 1967. See further Arendt.
Street, Harry & Frame, F R
  Law relating to nuclear energy. London 1966.
Sundström, G O Zacharias

The public international utility corporation. Helsinki 1971.

Three discussions on the conflict of laws. Uppsala 1970. (Acta Institutii Iuris prudentiae comparativae. XI)

Några komparativa och internationellt privaträttsliga synpunkter beträffande internationell handel. En studie i partshänvisningens effekt. Tidsskrift for Rettsvitenskap. 1966.

Wade, H W R

Administrative law. 3 ed. Oxford 1971.

Waline, Marchel

Précis de droit administratif. Paris 1971.

Traité de droit administratif. 8 ed. Paris 1958.

Wall, E H

The Court of Justice of the European Communities. Jurisdiction and procedure. London 1966.

Wigny, Pierre

Droit administratif. Bruxelles 1953.

Wortely, B A

Aspects of the 1951 Hague Conference on private international law. Festschrift Lewald. Basel 1953.

Bulletin of the European Communities.

Suppl. 4/72. "Rapport Vedel". Rapport du group ad hoc pour l'examen du problème de l'accroissement des compétence du parlement européen.

Suppl. 6/73. Orientations et actions prioritaires pour la politique énergétique communautaire.

Suppl. 9/73. Renforcement des pouvoirs du parlement européen en matière budgétaire.

Commission of the European Communities.

10070/IX/69. General terms and conditions governing supply contracts.

XIV/398/72 rev. 1. Preliminary draft convention on the law applicable to contractual and non-contractual obligations.

SEC (74) 2542 final. Energy for Europe.

Auditor's report for the year 1973 by Paul Gaudy. (ECSC.) Luxembourg 1974.

La Communauté européenne, aujourd'hui, demain. Paris 1973. (Bureau d'information des Communautés Européennes.)

General report of the activities of the EC in 1973. Seventh, Brussels 1974.

General report of the activities of the EC in 1974. Eight, Brussels 1975.

Les recours juridictionnels contre les actes administratifs spécialement economiques dans le droit des États membres de la CEE. Rapport final par J-M Auby assisté de M Fromont. Bruxelles 1971. (Collection étude. Serie Concurrence — Rapprochement des législations. No 12.)

Règlement financier du fonds européen de développement (1969) institué par l'accord interne relatif au financement et à la gestion des aides de la Communauté. Bruxelles 1971. (71/68/CEE.)

Council decision of 4 June 1974 on the establishment of the Joint Undertaking Hochtemperatur-Kernkraftwerk GmbH (HKG). (74/295/Euratom.) (O.J. No L 165/7. 20.6.74.)

Statut des fonctionnaires des CE & Régime applicable aux autres agents des Communautés. (O.J. C 100. 28.9.72.)

Convention concernant la competence judiciaire et l'exécution des décisions en matière civile et commerciale. 1968. & Protocol. 1971.

Convention de Yaoundé. II. L'association des pays et territoires d'outremer à la CEE. 1971.

Vienna convention on the Law of Treaties. 1969.

IAEA. Nuclear law for a developing world. Vienna 1969. (Legal series. No. 5.)

Colloque de droit nucléaire européen. 3. Paris 1965.

La responsabilité de l'Euratom. Colloque de droit nucléaire européen. Paris 1966.

QUEEN MARY COLLEGE
LIBRARY
MILE END ROAD,
LONDON, E.1.